BIS Publishers
Building Het Sieraad
Postjesweg 1
1057 DT Amsterdam
The Netherlands
T +31 (0)20 515 02 30
bis@bispublishers.com
www.bispublishers.com

ISBN 90 6369 444 9

BISPUBLISHERS

CEX SELLS

New inspiration for valuable customer experiences

PREFACE

In the summer of 2005 we became colleagues at VODW. Both consultants and both passionate about helping organizations to become more customer centric in the broadest sense: it was an obvious and easy match. Ever since, we've completed many projects in the field of customer experience for a vast array of organizations. Sometimes we worked together, sometimes we were in different teams, always challenging and inspiring each other to create the best customer experiences.

During the course of these projects, we shared our methodology with organizations on how to create distinctive customer experiences. Moreover, we found out that it was about more than sharing the methodology: they asked us about practical examples and best practices in other organizations which they can learn from and be inspired by.

Therefore, in 2015 we decided to create a book of inspiration. A book full of customer experience (CEX) cases that show something extraordinary and prove that a good customer experience really leads to better business results. CEX Sells was born. A book, written in Dutch, describing cases of organizations, which, in our view, do something inspiring which others can learn from.

Our first book led to this second book you are now holding. An international edition this time, to meet the many requests of organizations outside the Netherlands to inspire them, too. It includes thirty completely new cases since we have found many more inspiring customer experiences from organizations around us. Organizations worldwide, both B2B and B2C, across a broad spectrum of industries.

In addition to the fact that we had new cases, we also wanted to write a second book since the field of customer experience has has developed further in the past years. The expertise available is becoming more mature: marketing automation, predictive analytics, machine learning and robotization are nowadays crucial elements in the field of customer experience. Agile working within a customer experience ecosystem is a further key factor in the field. These are all elements that you'll come across in this book.

We hope that you and your organization draw a lot of inspiration from these pages so that, together, we can improve your customers' experiences. Not only for your customers, but also for you, since good customer experience is the key success factor of successful organizations. An experience that fits the brand, contributes to more loyal customers and more revenues, and which can result in lower operational costs at the same time. All in all, effective customer experience management directly leads to better business results. We proclaim: CEX Sells!

Deborah Wietzes and Beate van Dongen Crombags

TABLE OF CONTENTS

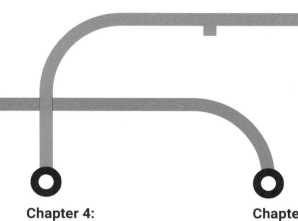

Chapter 4:
KEEP ON INNOVATING

How embracing new technologies and philosophies can speed up realizing better experiences 110

Chapter 5:
BYE BYE, CUSTOMER EXPERIENCE MANAGER

How to organize your customer experience management 144

Appendices

Chapter 1
CEX SELLS

HOW TO FIND THE BALANCE BETWEEN WHAT CUSTOMERS WANT AND WHAT YOUR ORGANIZATION NEEDS

We claim CEX Sells: a better customer experience leads to better business results. That means that an improvement in the customer experience should not only lead to higher customer satisfaction, but also to more sales, less churn and lower operating costs.

How can you ensure that you define how to improve your customer journey in such a way that it cuts both ways? This is the central question in the first chapter. First, let's start with a clear understanding of what we mean by a customer journey.

Customer journey: all touchpoints a customer has with your organization over time

The customer's overall experience of an organization comes down to the sum of all their individual experiences over time. For example, customer experience with an airline is commonly understood as referring to everything that happens during the flight. However, the experience already starts the moment a customer begins shopping around for a holiday and might even continue years after, upon recollection of this holiday. All these moments of contact combined are what we call the 'customer journey'.

Each contact moment, whether direct, for example through the website, or indirect, for example through reading reviews on a forum, can lead to a positive, negative or neutral customer attitude regarding the organization or brand. Plotting all points of contact and attitudes provides us with a clear picture of the current customer journey.

The customer journey measurement framework

Looking at all the contacts your customers have with your organization during the complete customer lifecycle, you need to do thorough research to define which moments to focus on. Qualitative research is often used to analyze the emotions customers have during their journey. For example by letting customers keep a diary, performing in-depth interviews or organizing focus groups, you get insight into what kind of contacts the customer encounters, what they feel, what they like and dislike and what could be improved. These last elements in particular can provide a mine of ideas for possible improvements: qualitative research often leads to long lists of possible actions. But where to start? As mentioned before, ideally you would like to start with those actions that are not only important to the customer, but also contribute to your business objectives. Analyzing this quantitative research is performed in addition to the qualitative research.

To measure the customer journey quantitatively, we distinguish six types of measurement.

Firstly, we distinguish between the measurements within one journey to compare contact moments, and measurements across journeys to compare journeys. 'Across journeys' could mean, for example, that we compare the journeys for buying a mobile phone with the journey for ending a TV contract for a telecom provider. But for this same provider, this could also mean we compare the mobile phone journey for students with the journey of families, as long as there are two or more journeys to compare.

Secondly, we recognize three dimensions you want to measure: the frequency, the experience and the impact.

This leads to six types of measurement. But that doesn't mean you would only need to manage six graphs on your customer experience dashboard. Sometimes, six graphs will not be enough: if you target several segments, for example retail customers and professionals, you want to have all measurements for each segment.

Let's discuss the six measurements one by one.

Frequency per contact moment

For each of the contact moments, you want to know at least how often they occur within one journey.

The frequency provides you with insights on the sales funnel: how many people go from one contact to the next step in the funnel? It also provides valuable information about the service contacts, especially when the frequency is measured per channel. How many contacts do we have in each channel? Do people use the right channels for the right contacts? These insights help you to manage the customer journey and give you an initial idea of which areas to focus on.

Most organizations have the data available and already measure given frequencies. Step by step, adding more contact moments to measure and ensuring you can split the frequencies per contact channel is the first phase in managing your customer experience.

Frequency per journey

When comparing frequencies over journeys, we can prioritize certain journeys over others. Maybe some service contacts occur more often by phone in one journey, while in another journey the customers find their answers online. What can we learn from the journey with more online contacts in order to migrate the service contacts in the other journey to the online channels as well? Or maybe the journey where people first get their welcome package and then call the contact center occurs more often? Now we know that the welcome package is provoking questions, we should change that. To be able to distinguish between the various contact moment sequences within journeys, you need to have a lot of data available on an individual level, both online and offline. It is not very common yet, but more and more organizations are moving in this direction. The analysis of the sequence of contact moments, so-called 'process mining' is discussed more elaborately in Chapter 3.

Figure 1.1 Six quantitative customer experience measurements

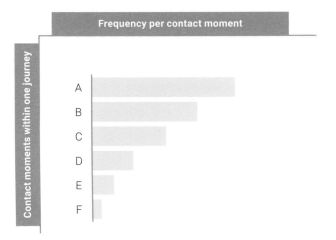

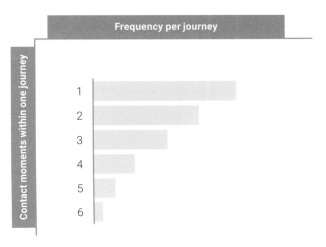

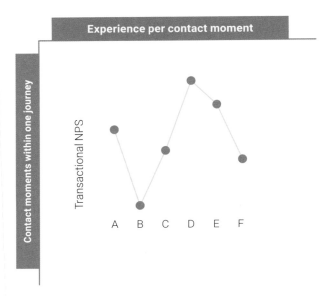

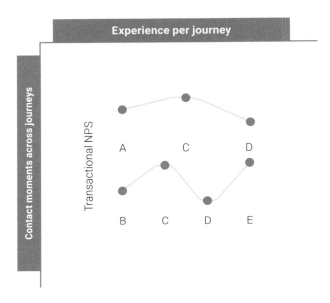

Experience per contact moment

One of the downsides of measuring only the frequency is that frequency says nothing about the experience. Maybe the contact moment or journey occurs a lot, but if you don't know if everybody likes it or hates it, it is still hard to take decisions based on this information. Therefore, you should measure the experience as well. Most organizations measure this with the transactional NPS, or Net Promoter Score: for a given contact moment, you ask a customer whether they would recommend you to their friends or colleagues based on that contact moment. This gives insight into the transactional Net Promoter Score and shows you which moments are positively or negatively evaluated. Some organizations don't measure the NPS, but customer satisfaction: they ask how satisfied the customer was with that contact moment, or the Customer Effort Score (CES), where they ask how easy it was for the customer to deal with their organization.

This kind of quantitative research is performed often nowadays and leads to an emotion curve as shown above.

Experience per journey

By comparing the emotion curves of different journeys, organizations can see whether some contact moments score extremely high or extremely low across journeys. This leads to insights in more generic optimizations: for example, if your service contacts score high in all journeys, you could use this as a unique selling point in communication. Or if the welcome package has a negative score in many journeys, you want to redesign this contact moment with high priority.

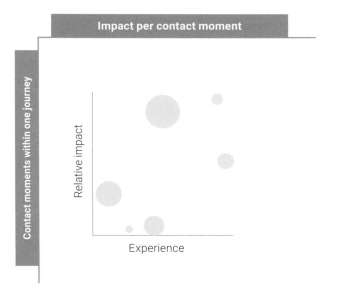

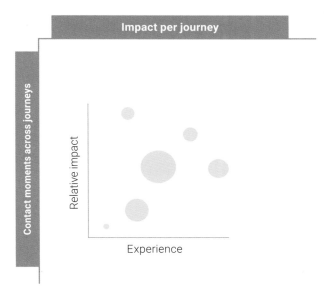

Impact per contact moment

To determine which contact moment should be changed first you need to have insights into the impact of a contact moment on the overall business objectives of your organization.

Ideally you have information on an individual level about which contact moments a customer has experienced and what the satisfaction score per contact moment is. If you also have information related to your business objective (for example information on whether a customer remained a customer for another year if loyalty is your objective) you can analyze the impact of each individual contact moment on the overall business objective continuously.

Unfortunately, you need a lot of data on an individual level, which is almost impossible to get. Therefore, we suggest performing yearly or half yearly surveys where you investigate all contact moments to discover the impact of each individual contact moment. For each one, you ask the respondent whether they have experienced the moment and how satisfied they were about that contact. After you have asked the satisfaction score for each possible contact moment, you ask a limited number of more global questions related to your main business KPIs. Would the customer recommend your organization to friends or colleagues if NPS is an important KPI? How much effort did the customer experience in doing business with your organization, if the CES is an important KPI?

Next to these KPIs, you should ask about the brand image the customer has of your organization based on the brand values. If a brand value is, for example, empathetic, you ask whether the customer thinks your organization is empathetic. In this way, you can analyze the impact of a contact moment on your brand image at the same time.

By using a combination of state-of-the-art econometric techniques, the relative impact of each touchpoint can now be related to the business KPIs and brand values.

Impact per journey

The same impact-defining methodology applies for measuring the impact across different journeys. Should you start with the journey for product X or for product Y? For private customers or for business partners? The journey for moving house or for payments? Comparing journeys helps you to prioritize contact moments across journeys and to set the right strategy per journey.

The customer experience impact matrix

The impact per contact moment or per journey can be demonstrated in what we call the 'customer experience impact matrix'. It plots all contact moments or journeys on both the customer satisfaction, that is, the experience, and the relative impact on business objectives. Moreover, the size of the dot indicates the number of respondents that say they have experienced that contact or journey (the frequency). The larger the dot, the more people experienced it. When prioritizing the contact moments or journeys, of course one that is experienced by more people will get a higher priority.

Now let's take a closer look at each quadrant (see figure 1.1) and the consequent strategy. Though we describe the strategies for the contact moments, assuming the customer experience impact matrix is made for one journey, the same applies for the customer journeys if the matrix is made for more journeys. Therefore, whenever we use the word 'moment', you can also read 'journey'.

Figure 1.2 The customer experience impact model

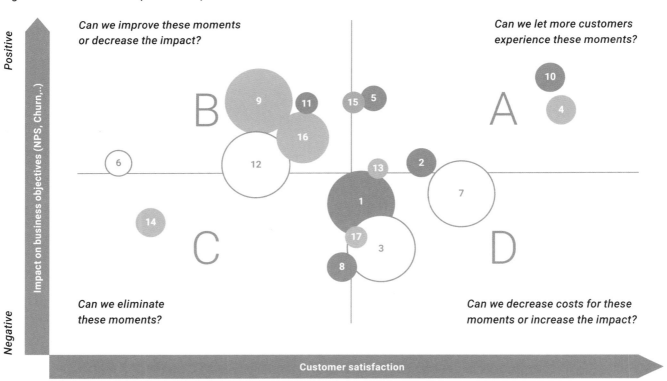

Moments with a high customer satisfaction score and positive impact on the KPIs

You can really set yourself apart from competitors with these moments. These are the moments that emphasize why customers have chosen and keep on choosing your organization over others. This positive impact can even be enlarged by ensuring more customers experience these moments. You can also let the positive experience resonate better. For example, by emphasizing these unique experiences in content marketing or in the customer service contacts.

 Moments with a low customer satisfaction score, yet a positive impact on the KPIs

Quite often, these are contact moments meant to simplify processes for your customers, however they do not yet meet expectations. Let's take banking apps. Online banking has already had a positive effect on the business KPIs, but apps increase the number of contacts, which therefore has a significant positive effect. Yet the usage of the app itself is often not entirely what the customer wants. This is in part due to the fact that customers' expectations towards apps are quite often set by experiences in other industries, which are not always easy to follow by large and slow banks. Continuously adding new functionalities and increasing the usability of apps increases the customer satisfaction and moves these contact moments from the upper left quadrant to the upper right one.

 Moments with a low customer satisfaction score and a negative impact on the KPIs

These moments are deadly for your customer experience! Customers are dissatisfied and this negatively influences your business objectives. Complaints are an obvious example, but also payments or newsletters can be found in this quadrant. In general, these are the contact moments customers did not ask for and therefore don't like.

The solution quite often is not in the contact moment itself, but in one or more of the previous moments. What caused this negative moment to happen? Is there any way we could have prevented this moment from happening?

Instead of optimizing these types of contact moments, you want to remove them. For example, by investigating what went wrong in the previous moments and changing that, or by minimizing the impact, e.g. by automating the process.

If you really can't change the moment itself or the previous moments, another way of limiting the impact is by immediately following up on the negative moment by a positive moment. That's why some organizations send flowers after a major complaint.

 Moments with a high customer satisfaction score, yet a negative impact on the KPIs

Good news: customer experience is not only about investing. It is about optimizing the resources you have and might mean you are investing in the wrong things, or even that you can save money.

Based on quantitative research, it sometimes turns out that a contact moment has a high customer satisfaction score but still has a negative impact on the business objectives. If you only look at the customer satisfaction score, you might think these moments are important assets to your organization. However, instead of maximizing the number of people that experience these moments, you want to minimize it. Or even diminish these moments completely, since during these moments you are apparently overdoing it: every time a customer experiences one of them, it negatively influences your KPIs.

Think about waiting time. Customers don't like to wait of course, so a lot of companies are investing to decrease waiting time. However, sometimes having to wait for a minute less might influence customer satisfaction, but not the business KPIs. Imagine the costs you could save by allowing a longer waiting time and accepting a lower satisfaction score for this contact moment. You can only do so if you know that this won't negatively influence the business objectives.

Next to savings, you can also investigate why these moments don't contribute to your KPIs; maybe a redesign could ensure they do.

By analyzing for each contact moment both the impact on the customer, i.e. customer satisfaction, and the impact on the

KPIs, that is the business objectives, you can balance what the customer wants and what your organization needs. You also can set different strategies for each contact moment to optimize the total customer experience.

Why not focus on the moments of truth?

Thus, we can distinguish between moments with limited impact, the 'standard moments', and 'moments of truth', with a high impact on the overall experience.

Of course, as an organization, you are looking for ways to optimize your customer journey. And since most organizations have limited resources, they focus on the moments of truth, as these have the highest impact. However, it is debatable whether this is the best approach to take. Let's consider three reasons why organizations should not solely focus on these high-impact moments.

1 *Moments of truth are equal for the whole industry*
The first disadvantage of solely focusing on moments of truth is the fact that these moments are just as important to you as they are to your competitors. Therefore, all your competitors will be focusing on them too. Take, for example, the car insurance industry. The biggest moment of truth for customers of a car insurer is the moment they submit a claim. After all, this moment results in them paying their significant monthly premiums for years on end. However, since this applies to all insurers, they all focus on optimizing this moment. This is therefore not the best moment for creating a competitive advantage as an organization.

2 *Moments of truth might not be the most important moments for your brand*
Let's stick to the example of the car insurer. If this insurer's brand values are all about protecting customers from any possible danger, then focusing on the moment of truth 'claim submission' is far less effective. Rather, a focus on all points of contact centered around protecting the customer from suffering any damage at all makes much more sense. Providing tips on upcoming bad weather and safe parking lots or giving discounts

on winter tires or parking assistance would probably be more in line with the brand values, leading to a greater competitive advantage. Of course, if the car insurer's brand values are all about accountability or helping you out in times of need, the claims moment might still be important to focus on. Therefore, we're not saying that you should never focus on moments of truth. However, we do wish to highlight, in addition to the impact for the customer, the importance of considering the impact on the business when defining the moments that really define your customer experience.

What are the moments where you really make a difference based on your unique brand values? What are your 'branded moments'?

3 *Moments of truth are not generic. Different customers have different moments of truth*
Research shows that the impact of a touch point might differ for different types of customer. What is important to one person might be less important to another. Even for one single person, the impact might differ depending on the situation.

To illustrate this, let's get back to our car insurer. Some customers might have done extensive research to find good insurance at the lowest premium possible. When these customers see their quote, this constitutes a moment of truth: is the premium really lower than that of the competitors? Other customers might be willing to pay a higher premium, if this means they get better coverage in return. For them, the moment of truth is not so much seeing the quote, as it is reading the insurance policy.

However, reading the insurance policy might become a moment of truth for the first group of customers as well, as soon as they have an accident and discover they are not covered for that kind of damage. This changes their situation, suddenly turning something that seemed irrelevant at first into a moment of truth. Organizations that really know their customers and focus on optimizing each individual customer journey will truly create a bond with these customers, leading to the best competitive advantage.

Thus, next to defining the impact of a contact moment, we also need to consider our brand values and the different types of customer. These will be discussed in the following chapters.

Key take-aways:

- The customers' overall experience of an organization comes down to the sum of all their individual experiences over time.
- Do not only measure the frequency of a contact moment, but also the experience.
- Define the impact of individual moments on the overall objectives of your organization.
- Be aware of the relative impact of each single touch point related to the business KPIs and brand values.
- Do not solely focus on the 'moments of truth'.

THE ROYAL CONCERTGEBOUW & NETHERLANDS PHILHARMONIC ORCHESTRA

Combining data to optimize the concert experience

The Royal Concertgebouw, which in English translates to 'concert building', opened in Amsterdam on 11 April 1888 and has been considered one of the best concert halls in the world ever since due to its fine acoustics.

With the Royal Concertgebouw Orchestra, the Netherlands Philharmonic Orchestra and its partner, the Netherlands Chamber Orchestra, it is one of the most regular performers at the Royal Concertgebouw. The Netherlands Philharmonic Orchestra or NedPhO for short, is renowned for making classical music accessible to a broad audience and for enabling extraordinary experiences, for example giving the audience the opportunity to meet the musicians.

How can one create the best concert experience?

NedPhO wants to make a visit to their concerts a memorable experience. It not only ensures the concert itself is appreciated by the audience, but also spends a lot of time thinking about what it can do before or after the concert to enhance the experience.

Data is an important source of information in order to do so. NedPhO combines its own data with data from the Royal Concertgebouw and external statistical data to get a complete view of its visitors. Different customer profiles can be found, based on address, age, music genre and buying behavior. NedPhO identified eight different segments with different journeys. For example, the hard-core visitors who want to be informed of the new season as soon as possible by post and order the complete ticket series via the post, e-mail or phone. Or the one-time visitor from Amsterdam who hears or reads about single concerts via social media or in magazines and buys tickets not more than four weeks in advance.

NedPhO adjusts the different customer journeys based on these profiles: the moment the ticket sales start, the people to focus on and the media to use. But it also gives new insights into the optimal program for the concerts themselves.

Measuring in order to define the moments with the most impact

Frequent research is carried out by the Royal Concertgebouw to gather insights into the complete concert experience. It measures what visitors think about the different elements of their concert visit. Next to what the visitor thinks of these elements, i.e. the impact for the visitor, the importance of each element related to the visitor's decision to return is measured (the impact of the concert hall and its performers). In this way, a customer experience impact matrix as previously described in this chapter is created. This leads to interesting insights. The cloakroom, for example, is something that often has low scores, since people need to wait to get their coats after the concert. Yet this only has limited impact on the probability of returning.

However, an element that is highly appreciated and has a strong impact for potential future visits is the 'side programming'. For example, NedPhO wants to connect the visitors to the concert by offering an introduction beforehand. The artistic manager of NedPhO gives an explanation about the different themes of the concert at the concert hall's café prior to the performance, so visitors can better recognize these themes while it takes place. For frequent visitors, this is not always of additional value, since they already know the themes. But for this group, NedPhO organizes 'pre-concert talks', where visitors have the chance to meet the soloists, conductors and musicians in person before the concert. Also, after the concert the side programming continues. In one of the foyers of the Concertgebouw, the visitors can share a drink while listening to the musicians from the orchestra playing different music to what they would normally play (jazz, country, chansons, etc).

With NedPhO 30, the orchestra started a new form of side-programming focusing on a specific target group. This new initiative focuses on creating social events around the concerts for younger visitors (up to the age of 30).

New innovations to improve the experience

One of the latest modernizations to improve the concert experience during the concert is an app where you can follow the performance on your smartphone. With this app, named 'Wolfgang', you can read a short explanation of the different parts of the concert and the symbolism used. It is like having subtitles for the concert. With Wolfgang, the visitor better understands the performance and, especially for non-frequent visitors, this increases the appreciation of the concert. Approximately 10% of all visitors use the app during the concert, and the other visitors are not disturbed so it is a win-win.

NedPhO, together with the concert hall, is also looking for new ways to change the lighting for different parts of concerts to enhance the experience.
Last but not least, the orchestra is of course itself responsible for a huge part of the overall experience. The sound quality of its performances is what makes it one of the most popular orchestras in the Netherlands. However, NedPhO is also thinking about its image. Special attention is paid to the way the players dress, with just as much attention to the way they look overall. They need to give the right energy to the public and show they are enjoying themselves, to ensure the public is enjoying itself too.

What your organization can learn from the Royal Concert building and NedPhO:

- Combine your data with partners in your ecosystem to create enriched profiles and thus better insights into the customer journey.
- Differentiate the different segments and measure the customer journey per segment.
- Do not only measure customer satisfaction to focus on the elements with the lowest score, but also add the impact on the business objective (in this case, a future visit) to truly focus on the elements with the biggest impact.
- Make sure you map the total customer journey. Where does this start and where does this end from a customer's point of view?

AUSTRALIAN AND NEW ZEALAND BANKING GROUP

Mapping the journey

combining facts and feelings

ANZ, the Australian and New Zealand Banking Group, is one of the leading banks in both countries. ANZ provides commercial and retail banking and financial services to about eight million customers in 33 nations worldwide. ANZ services their customers via traditional channels at branches, ATMs and contact centers, but is now seen as one of the frontrunners moving into the digital field with online and mobile banking apps as well.

21 building blocks to become a customer service leader

For ANZ, just like all banks, a good customer experience is key. Products are quite similar, so differentiating oneself in the market is all about providing the most customer friendly customer journey.

ANZ started a big customer experience program to put the customer in the center of everything they do. By doing so, ANZ wanted to create more insightful and connected customer experience throughout the customer journey.

The first step was to map the current customer experience. ANZ performed face-to-face interviews to get qualitative insights, but also used all data internally available to strengthen these insights with quantitative facts.

About 70 ANZ representatives from different departments were invited to a three-day workshop to discuss the current experience. In this workshop, representatives from partners of ANZ were also included and, of course, customers were part of the workshop too. ANZ made a clear selection of customers representing the different segments of ANZ and the different contact channels offered by ANZ.

The workshop led to a clear view on the current experience, as well as to 21 building blocks to become a customer service leader.

Feedback program to measure improvements and empower sales

The building blocks give ANZ a clear focus on what to improve. But ANZ understands that simply implementing the 21 building blocks isn't enough to continuously deliver the best customer experience in the long run. Once they had mapped the current customer journeys, they wanted to keep track of this, both to measure the effect of the improvements made, and to find new areas to focus on.

The commercial effect of the improvements could already be measured by the current information systems, but ANZ was not yet systematically measuring the customer experience. Therefore, ANZ implemented a feedback program. Customers now receive short questionnaires after having contact with the bank.

This enables ANZ to measure the effect of each individual improvement. It also enables ANZ to take immediate action if the feedback gives any reason for this. This could be an internal action, e.g. if there is a typo on the website, but more importantly, action towards the customer. ANZ found out that the feedback program in itself also has a positive effect on the customer experience and the sales. Customers like the fact that ANZ asks them for their feedback and acts on this. Real-time insights help ANZ to continuously find new areas to improve. It shows customers' likes and dislikes and gives concrete ideas on how to improve the customer experience. Nonetheless, ANZ does not simply take the customer feedback and starts changing things. Before any new app, new functionality, new content or any other customer facing change is launched, ANZ performs customer research to ensure the improvement is completely in line with customer needs.

Data-driven insights for personal and relevant conversations

Another important element of delivering the best customer experience is ensuring every contact is perfectly attuned to the customer. The insights from the customer feedback are used to train the employees with direct contact to better serve their customers. To support these employees, ANZ invested in data and analytical skills to have the right conversations at the right time.

ANZ owns a lot of customer data. Think about all the log-ins on the banking app, the contacts with the contact centers or via the branches, or the use of debit or credit cards. ANZ combines contact data, product data and transactional data and adds behavioral and socioeconomic data to that. By using a mix of analytical techniques, a lot of information can be derived from this data. ANZ gets a deeper understanding of who their customers are and what their customer journey with ANZ looks like.

Previously, ANZ only analyzed this data monthly, but ANZ has now moved to real-time insights. And these insights are available to the people that can act on them and who can now use the information to make all conversations personal and relevant to the customer. Think about an SMS regarding payments abroad once ANZ detects a customer is using their credit card abroad. Or an interesting cross- or up-sell offer at the branch or in marketing campaigns based on the customer's behavior ('next best action' conversations). Another example of using these real-time analytics is on the website. Once the customer has logged on to internet banking, ANZ recognizes them and tailors the website real-time for the type of customer they are and the search patterns they show on the website.

Structuring all data also led to new possibilities to optimize processes. A good example of this is the fact that ANZ customers can continue to use their digital wallet (either Apple Pay or Android Pay) when their credit card is lost or stolen. Once ANZ gets notified about this, they automatically update the card details of the new card in the digital wallet.

What your organization can learn from ANZ:

- Thorough customer research helps you to identify the areas to focus on and improve.
- Real-time insights allow you to optimize the customer experience real-time.
- Adding external data will lead to a richer customer profile and therefore to deeper customer insights.
- Invest heavily in your data skills: you need them in this digital era.
- A good customer feedback program leads to an improvement in sales.

GAS NATURAL FENOSA

Put the customer first

Gas Natural Fenosa is a global energy group and has its headquarters in Barcelona. Although the group primarily operates in Spain, it is active in over 30 countries worldwide, including Italy, France, Mexico, Argentina and Morocco. Gas Natural Fenosa's core business lies in the regulated and liberated gas and electricity markets, serving close to 23 million customers worldwide. Customer orientation is an important value for the company and it strives to provide customers with an excellent service.

A customer experience program to create emotional bonding with customers

Gas Natural Fenosa recently started a customer experience program to create an emotional bond with its customers. These customers and their needs are the starting point for the cultural change within Gas Natural Fenosa.

The objectives of the customer orientation are threefold:

- Firstly, Gas Natural Fenosa keeps on working to improve their products and services. The company wants to continuously differentiate itself by ensuring these products and services are tailored to the needs of its customers. They continuously innovate by extending the range of products and services and so deliver on a broader set of customer needs.
- Gas Natural Fenosa understands that they are not the only actor in delivering the optimal customer experience. Several suppliers are key for success and therefore the company focuses on creating and maintaining long-term relationships with these suppliers. They are part of a larger ecosystem (see Chapter 5).
- The biggest change derived from the program is the true focus on the customers, by giving them a voice within the organization. Customers' opinions are the starting point of the design and development of functionalities, contact channels, campaigns etc. The program positions the customer at the center of all the decision-making activities within the organization.

Gas Natural Fenosa sees today's customer as a person looking for experiences and who sets preferences via the recommendations of others. Therefore, Gas Natural Fenosa believes that by incorporating the needs of the customer in everything they do, this will not only improve customer satisfaction but also increase customer recommendations. And this will lead to a competitive advantage. And with success! In the first year, Gas Natural Fenosa's Net Promoter Score increased by 80% and sales also increased significantly.

Worldwide customer experience measurement as an integral part of the total service offering

Customers contacting Gas Natural Fenosa are asked how satisfied they are with the response provided and how likely it is that they would recommend the company. This kind of customer experience management tool might not be so special, but Gas Natural Fenosa added an alert system to this. Whenever the minimum satisfaction score or the minimum recommendation level as required by the company is not reached, an alert is activated. The company follows up on all cases where the customer says that they would not recommend Gas Natural Fenosa in order to understand why the customer is disappointed, and learn how this could be improved. Based on this feedback, action plans are developed to improve the customer experience.

Another inspiring element is the fact that Gas Natural Fenosa uses new technologies to encourage ongoing contact between the customer and the company. On the mobile app for example, the customer can easily manage their account frequently and share feedback. But social networks also play an important role in understanding the customer.

These insights are not only shared within the departments with direct contacts to the customer. The whole customer experience program is company-wide. Both departments with direct links to the customer and the departments behind the scenes understand the program and how they can contribute. Furthermore, the program is global: the customer experience department within Gas Natural Fenosa ensures the cultural change from operational excellence to customer centricity on a global level by standard methodologies and the exchange of international best practice.

What your organization can learn from Gas Natural Fenosa:

- True customer focus leads to improved business results. Ensure the customer is at the center of everything you do.
- Measure customer experience after each interaction to get a complete view of what is important to the customer and what is not. Ensure follow-up for remarkable cases!
- Share customer insights with the whole organization so everyone can act on them.
- Ensure the cultural change is organization-wide, in all departments and all countries.
- Use all customer touchpoints to start conversations with your customers and create strong relationships.

CLEVELAND CLINIC

Operating a truly patient-centered organization is a way of life

The academic hospital located in Cleveland, Ohio, is nationally recognized as one of the best clinics worldwide. The Cleveland Clinic was established in 1921 and has pioneered many procedures and made breakthrough discoveries ever since. Cleveland Clinic is one of the largest non-profit health care providers in the United States, operating one of the largest hospitals in the US, several community hospitals and family health centers as well as specialized centers in Florida and Las Vegas and operations in Canada, Abu Dhabi and Saudi Arabia.

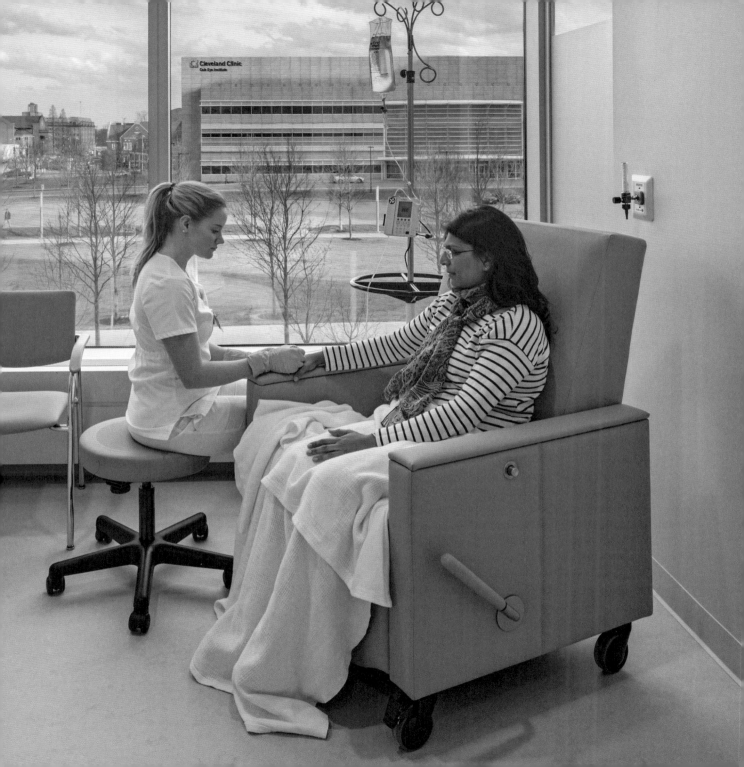

Patient journey to combine operational excellence and customer focus

The Cleveland Clinic has long had a reputation for medical excellence and for keeping costs down.

However, since 2010 the clinic decided to take up customer-centricity as a strategic theme as well.

Until then, Cleveland Clinic was mainly focused on medical outcomes. For one of the best hospitals such as Cleveland Clinic, this is naturally the main priority. The customer journey, or in this case the patient journey, was not taken into account. Touchpoints such as making an appointment, offering a pleasant environment, truly understanding the customer's emotions and providing clear information were not a priority, whereas medical excellence was.

Yet Cleveland Clinic saw they were lagging behind in the area of customer experience and made it a strategic priority. They now strive to have the best customer reputation, next to the best medical reputation.

Seven radical changes for extreme customer focus:

One: The clinic established a thorough understanding of the patients' needs

Though the medical experts thought only medical outcomes mattered, customer research showed a lot of patients were dissatisfied by the services offered. Additional research showed the root causes and deeper understanding of this dissatisfaction. Based on both qualitative and quantitative research, some surprising insights were collected. First of all, patients did not want to be in hospital. Emotions such as being afraid, or even terrified, confusion and anxiety should be taken into consideration by all employees of the hospital, as concerns both patients and their families.

Another factor to be improved was communication. Communication between doctors was so poor that the patient felt like no one was taking care of them. Also, communication towards the patient could be improved. The patient wants to know what is going on every second of their stay at the hospital.

A third element that came up was the role of the carers. If they were happy, the patient tended to give a higher satisfaction score for the hospital.

Two: The clinic made each employee a carer

The relation between the patient and the doctor is considered by the hospital to be the most important relationship. However, for the patient all interactions are important. Everyone at Cleveland Clinic, from nurses to surgeons, from physicians to concierges, was trained to take the patient as the main starting point and put them first. The program showed each profession what they could do to improve the patient experience.

Three: The clinic increased employee engagement

The Cleveland Clinic started a 'caregiver celebration' program, allowing both managers and frontline workers to recognize colleagues who had done something exceptional for patients or for the clinic. This recognition program consists both of financial rewards as well as acknowledgment during the annual ceremony.

Four: The clinic established new processes

Of course, measuring the patient experience is not a one-off exercise. The clinic implemented processes, created metrics, and monitored performance, receiving continuous insights into what was already good and what could be improved. A special best practices department was appointed, to pilot possible improvements and roll them out once proven successful. One of the initiatives from this was a single dedicated phone number for booking appointments. This made the Cleveland Clinic the first major hospital in the US to give all patients the option of getting an appointment on the same day they call. When patients call this number, agents answer the phone with: "Thank you for calling the Cleveland Clinic. Would you like to be seen today?"

*Five: The clinic increased collaboration
by introducing multidisciplinary teams*

The clinic introduced institutes in which multidisciplinary teams treat all the conditions affecting a particular organ system, for example its heart and vascular institute.
This new care model improved collaboration and increased quality while at the same time reducing costs. Moreover, it improved patient experience.

Six: The clinic set patients' expectations.

With printed materials and interactive videos, the Cleveland Clinic now communicates intensively with patients about what is going to happen, how long each step will take and what they can expect.

*Seven: The clinic appointed a chief experience
officer to drive the change*

The clinic put one person in charge of the patient experience. This Chief Experience Officer manages the 'Office of Patient Experience', which currently has a $9.2 million annual budget and 112 people in it, including project managers, data experts, and service excellence trainers. They ensure the patient experience is continuously measured and analyzed and improvements are being implemented.

Operational excellence and customer centricity go hand in hand

Though some medical experts were a bit cynical upfront, thinking the initiative would conflict with efforts to maintain high quality and further reduce costs, the program proved them wrong. The hospital is improving the patient experience, while medical excellence is rising as well. A success factor is the fact that the clinic put one person in charge of the patient experience.

What your organization can learn from the Cleveland Clinic:

- You don't have to choose between having the best processes and the best experience: you can have both.
- Happy carers ensure higher customer satisfaction in the clinic.
- Continuously measure the experience to keep on improving from a customer's point of view.
- Making all employees responsible for the customer experience increases the effect.
- Share best practices and put them in the spotlight to put the customer first in the whole organization.
- Multidisciplinary teams increase efficiency and the experience.
- Appoint a 'chief experience officer' to speed up the desired change.

UNILEVER

Orchestrating the complete hair care journey based on real-time insights

The British-Dutch consumer goods company Unilever owns over 400 brands, split into four divisions: foods, refreshments, homecare and personal care. Globally well-known brands include Becel/Flora, Omo, Knorr, Lipton and Magnum. In the area of hair care, Unilever is behind several brands, such as Dove, Tresemme, Nexxus, Aviance, Andrelon, Clear. Being one of the largest media buyers in the world, Unilever is always looking for new ways to optimize its marketing efforts and thereby improve the buying journey for their products.

Google data as a starting point to create relevant hair journeys

Based on Google data, Unilever found that its hair care customers search for hair care information over 11 billion times per year. That's about 30 million searches every single day. Unilever partnered with Google to use all information coming from these searches to gain real-time insights into what kind of information their target audience is looking for right now. This includes the kind of problems they face, the kind of questions, popular styles etc.

Unilever could have used this data at product level to optimize the customer journey for a certain brand, or maybe several brands separately. However, the data was not related to products, but to customer's needs. Therefore, Unilever decided to define a journey around hair care where all their brands should play a role, depending on the needs of the customers at that moment. Unilever set itself the target to have the complete hair care journey online and started 'all things hair' (ATH), a branded YouTube channel focusing on hair care through high-quality video content.

On the channel, popular and up-coming vloggers (video bloggers), show how you can treat your hair, style it, wash it etc. From party hairstyles to 1920's inspired curly hairstyles, to how to get great hair volume to hairstyles for a professional look. The actual content shown depends on the real-time Google searches at that moment and on trend predictions; only the most relevant information is shown and the customer always gets the most valuable customer journey. Unilever proves that using big data cleverly truly ensures you are relevant and useful to your customers.

Vloggers produce an important part of the content

As mentioned, next to big data, Unilever also improves the customer experience by using influencers. The vloggers are people within the ecosystem of the target audience. They are paid by Unilever, they are carefully selected and many of them have millions of followers in their own right too. For example Zoella, whose familiar and personal approach to make-up tutorials has led to over 11 million subscribers to her YouTube channel.

The combination of big data and the flexible vloggers is a key success factor for the best hair care journey. The vloggers respond quickly to increasing search terms or to trending topics, for example, a celeb's hairstyle at an awards show. Since the vloggers are truly helping the customer, they remain authentic. And though they are not pushing the products, the vloggers do explain the products they are using. It will not be a surprise to you that these are all Unilever products. Customers are encouraged to visit the ATH website via the YouTube channel to get more tips. Here, Unilever has the option to prominently show the products used and add links to the websites of these products where the customer can find more information.

The channel is national, showing the most relevant content of a certain region, keeping in mind the cultural differences between countries. Unilever initially started ATH in three countries, but there are a dozen different channels right now, with more to come. ATH quickly became the leading branded YouTube channel for hair care worldwide. All channels combined have generated over 65 million views since the launch in December 2013. On average, a visitor remains on the channel for almost 2 minutes. Think about how much media exposure you have to buy to get the same kind of attention.

What your organization can learn from Unilever:

- Do not define the customer journey based on the products you have, but on the needs your target audience has.
- Use not only your own data, but also external data to better manage your customer journey.
- Make each customer journey relevant to impacting your customer.
- Find the right partners in your ecosystem to maximize the impact on your business objectives.
- Take cultural differences into account.
- Find the right partners in your ecosystem to maximize the impact on your business objectives and do not only think about big organizations, but also about vloggers for example.

TROV

Optimizing the journey based on usage data

Trov is an American technology company focusing on on-demand insurance. Trov is the first insurer to let customers buy coverage just for the items they want, for example electronic devices or bicycles, and for a specific amount of time, entirely on the phone. Trov partnered with the Australian Insurer Suncorp Group to launch the platform in Australia in May 2016 and since September 2016, Trov is also available in the UK through a partnership with AXA. Thanks to new partnerships with Munich Re and Sompo Japan Nipponkoa, Trov will expand to more countries in the short term.

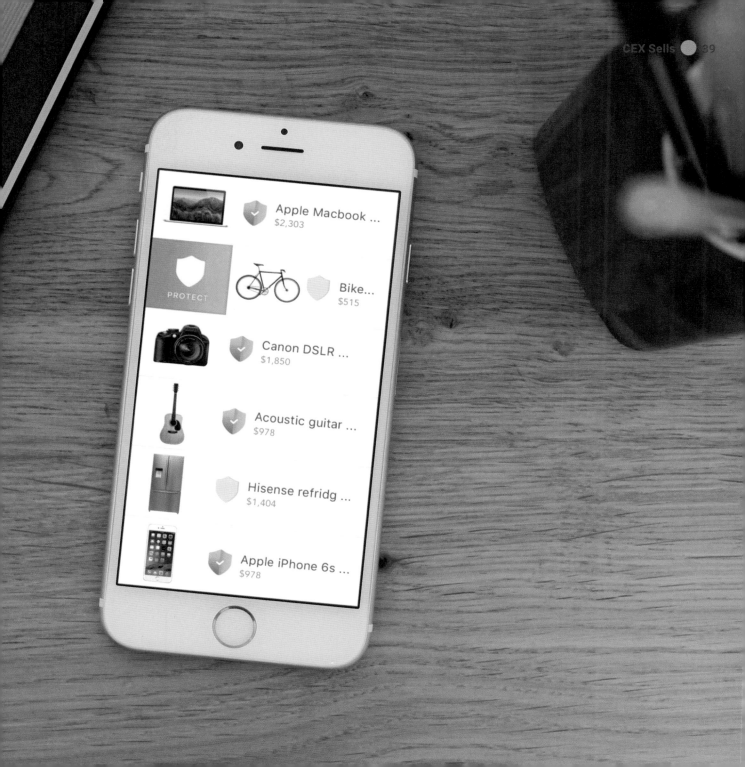

Apple Macbook ...
$2,303

PROTECT

Bike...
$515

Canon DSLR ...
$1,850

Acoustic guitar ...
$978

Hisense refridg ...
$1,404

Apple iPhone 6s ...
$978

Mobile only is a nice ambition, but Trov customers demand multichannel

Trov wants it customers to easily switch on and off what they want to cover. So Trov created an on-demand insurance app to enable this.

Within the app, customers can easily select what they want to cover by sharing the make and model, and select for how long they want to have it covered. The customer will get an immediate quote for a daily, weekly, monthly or annual premium. And even smarter, the app is able to detect instantly what kind of phone you have and immediately offers you a quote to protect your phone.

Trov created a great end-to-end mobile experience: automatic data collection helps the customer easily create a digital inventory of the things they own so the customer can just create a list with their possessions and simply turn protection on or off by swiping the button. The moment the coverage is turned on, these items are covered against damage, loss and theft. Customers can also easily take a photo of the item they want to cover, take a photo of the receipt or scan the barcode and everything is conveniently stored in their 'Trov', their own virtual vault in the cloud. In case anything does go wrong, the customer can select the item concerned and swipe to file a claim via the in-app chatbot, if needed backed-up with live chat with an agent.

An ideal mobile customer experience, however, by constantly measuring the sales funnel, Trov found out that a lot of customers start their insurance journey in a web browser. Though Trov. com provides clear and attractive information about the app, customers still have to download the app first and create an account, complete the information and find the right product to cover before they can really see the benefits of Trov. Based on this insight, Trov decided to create a web version as well. So now customers can have the same experience in the web browser, though they are still incited to download the app at a later stage, for their own convenience. And even better, Trov creates product-specific online ads to attract a group of

customers, e.g. photographers. When they click on the add, they immediately land on a specific page about covering their camera. As you can imagine, this combination of web and app increases conversion.

Continuous improvement to make the journey as simple as possible

Trov is constantly measuring and optimizing the track of the journey, as well as the content of the journey. By measuring the types of items customers want to cover, Trov gets a lot of insights on what products to put in the shortlist to select from. Trov frequently adds new product categories.

Moreover, its back-end is optimized every 2 weeks and its front-end, every month. And Trov is expanding the journey to the check-out of retailers. Retailers get the opportunity to embed Trov in the purchase process. Data from what you just bought is immediately added to your Trov and a quote is created directly: no action is needed from the customer. And if you don't have a Trov yet, you'll get an e-mail saying that the new product can be easily protected by simply downloading the app. Another new innovation soon to be added is a protection based on lifestyle. Trov understands customers do not only want to cover their camera, but the whole backpack with all the photography equipment in it. So customers will soon simply be able to turn on 'packages'. And GPRS data enables Trov to detect whenever you are traveling, so they can easily remind you to turn the coverage on.

Trov attracts millennials since they understand them. Millennials love to use their phones. All insurance companies know that, but most of them struggle to actually reach the younger generation. So they simply take their traditional products, with no specific items covered and with annual premiums, and offer them via an app. Trov is the first company to really use the benefits of mobile to create a type of insurance millennials love. Say you love to travel and take high quality pictures; a traditional insurer might be able to give you insurance for this, but then you have to go through a very specific and time-consuming process with strict underwriting, leading to a tailor-made insurance policy with a full-year premium. With Trov, this person only has to pay during the holidays when the policy is switched on. Now the millennials really get the control they want.

And it works: Trov is growing by about 44% every month.

What your company can learn from Trov:

- Target a specific audience and make sure you tailor the customer experience to their needs.
- Measuring the different paths within the omni-channel journey helps you to create better omni-channel experiences.
- Ensure the journey can easily be adjusted when you notice you need to add or change items.
- When using new channels in your journey, do not simply move the current journey to that channel but think how the specific characteristics of that channel can be used to improve the total experience.
- Think about the total customer journey for the customer and partner with other companies in that journey to optimize the total experience for the customer.

Chapter 2

DARE TO STAND OUT

HOW TO TRANSLATE YOUR BRAND VALUES INTO DISTINCTIVE EXPERIENCES

In the previous chapter, we have discussed the balance between customer wishes and business objectives. We believe the most important organization asset for achieving this are the brand values. Having clear brand values and being able to define 'brand moments' to create unique experiences for your customers ensures you will attract the customers that fit your brand. These same customers will be more enthusiastic about the product and services you offer, will buy more, stay longer and are more likely to become ambassadors of your brand.

Where is the love?

Please note that we talk about brand values, which are not to be confused with core values.

Core values are about *what* an organization does, brand values are about *how* they do it.

Core values are the values important to an organization and define the type of role it wants to play and how all employees should act. They are often generic, e.g. customer-oriented, market-leadership oriented, reliable.

Brand values define what kind of experience the customer should have while having contact with your organization; most companies have a clear set of brand values.

Quite often values such as 'transparent', 'easy', 'accessible', 'reliable' or 'fast' feature among an organization's brand values. Perfect brand values, but in our view more hygiene factors than drivers for distinctiveness.

The technological era we live in leads to high customer demands on your processes: customers expect many organizations to be accessible 24/7, to be able to take care of their businesses online, to respond to any inquiries within minutes, etc.

But all your competitors are striving for these perfect processes as well. So how can you remain distinct?

In this world where digitization is everywhere, consumers are looking for organizations that ensure a human touch. Though processes should be perfect, treating each customer as an individual makes the real difference. Taking their personal situation into account, understanding what they need, and showing you care about them. Processes become subordinate to feelings, campaigns change into conversations and standardization is balanced with tailor-made experiences.

Instead of only focusing on functional brand values, leading to functional benefits to customers, we believe the real competitive advantage is in defining the right emotional brand values. Emotional benefits will set you apart from competitors, lead to memorable customer experiences and will thus have a higher impact on your business objectives. We do not say processes don't matter, and we do not encourage you to neglect new technologies or data opportunities. On the contrary!

Especially if these can support you in optimizing the customer journey. But make sure you use them as a means to an end, not as a goal on their own. Balance between standard, generic processes and the personal touch when translating your brand values into customer experience.

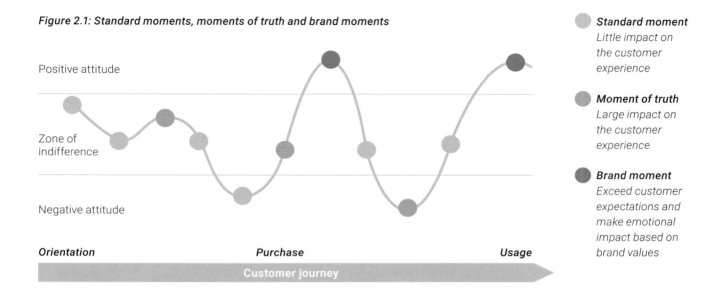

Figure 2.1: Standard moments, moments of truth and brand moments

Standard moment
Little impact on the customer experience

Moment of truth
Large impact on the customer experience

Brand moment
Exceed customer expectations and make emotional impact based on brand values

Why brand values like 'transparency' and 'reliable' won't lead to distinctive experiences

Organizations quite often perform customer research to find new areas of opportunity. They collect customer insights, define dislikes and untapped needs and improve the customer experience by implementing customer feedback. But organizations regularly forget to take their brand values into account while designing these improved or new experiences. These improvements may then lead to better experiences, but not always to distinctive experiences. By matching customer insights with your brand values, you create experiences that strengthen the image of your organization. You create what we call 'branded experiences'. Your unique signature should be experienced by the customer throughout the customer journey. At every contact with your organization, whether this is via telephone, the website, in a branch or a campaign, the customer should feel the same brand values.

Brand moments to create branded experiences
As stated before, this will not only lead to a consistent customer experience, but moreover to a competitive advantage; assuming your brand values are distinctive, they lead to distinctive experiences.

In Chapter 1 we explained the different emotions a customer might have during a customer journey: positive, negative or neutral. We explained the difference between 'standard moments' (with little impact on your customer experience) and 'moments of truth' (with high impact on your customer experience).

If, during a given contact moment, the customer clearly experiences your brand values – so that this is truly a different experience than a customer would have during the same contact moment with one of your competitors – these moments are key for your brand. We therefore call them brand moments.

Figure 2.2 The pyramid of contact moments

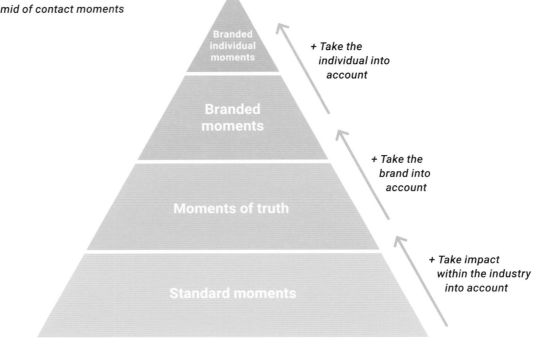

Brand moments are specific to your organization: during these moments, you want to create an emotional bond with your customers: you really want to connect to them in a unique way, in line with your brand values and thereby exceeding the customer's expectations.

This moment could be a moment of truth: an insurer, for example, could decide to exceed their customer's expectations during the claim moment. But a brand moment could also be a standard moment, for example by surprising the customer when sending the monthly invoice.

You could also decide to create a whole new contact moment, e.g. by contacting all customers who have been a customer with your organization for over ten years.

No matter whether this is a standard moment, a moment of truth or a new moment, once you decide this moment is a brand moment, it should lead to positive experiences.

Some organizations strive to be distinctive at every contact. In our view this is only possible for the so-called 'challenger brands': newcomers in the industry that can define their total customer experience from scratch. They have the resources and don't have to deal with old legacies. Think of companies such as Uber and Netflix.

Branded individual moments

Let's summarize: we started by making the distinction between standard moments and moments of truth. As stated in this chapter, we definitely need to take our brand values into account, leading to branded moments. Are branded moments the most valuable moments then?
In our view, one important dimension is still missing: the individual!
Who is experiencing the contact with your organization? In what kind of context and situation is he or she? What are his or her needs now? We are convinced that it is most effective for organizations to focus on branded individual moments. In order to be valuable to your organization the branded individual moments should be RICH:

- **R**eflecting the brand values.
- **I**ndividualizing the experience.
- **C**ontributing to the business objectives.
- **H**armonizing the customer journey as a whole.

Reflect the brand values

With brand values, an organization creates the image of the company. This unique signature should be experienced by the customer throughout the customer journey. This will not only lead to better customer experiences, but also to a competitive advantage.

Individualize the experience

What valuable means might differ from person to person and according to the situation?
So we need to know when it is relevant to a specific customer in a specific situation and to act on that.

Contribute to the business objectives

Valuable experiences are not only valuable to the customer, but also to the company.
It goes without saying that excellent customer experiences lead to higher customer satisfaction and NPS. So, if this is your main business objective, the two go hand in hand automatically. But what if your business objective is sales growth?

Or cross-selling? Or cost-saving? A clear understanding of the business objectives ensures you focus on these experiences that are beneficial both to your customers and to your business.

Harmonize the total customer journey

No single customer contact stands on their own. Customers have different contacts during different moments via different channels. Since the total customer experience is the sum of all these contacts, consistency is key. Only if you ensure a contact is perfectly in line with the other contacts, does this contact add value to the total experience.

How branded utilities can get you out of the commodity trap

A lot of industries are increasingly becoming commodity markets. Think of the insurance industry, the energy market or telecom industry. But also among consumer goods, products are more and more alike. So, buying decisions are mainly driven by price or ease of purchase.
Since it is harder to stand out solely through the product, organizations should try to be different through the customer experience. As mentioned above, branded experiences are key in order to differentiate oneself in homogeneous markets.
The key question is: will customers have enough contacts with your company to experience these distinctive, branded experiences? As an example, an insurance company will in general only have contacts with their customers at the moment of purchase and when the customer has a claim. To truly get out of the commodity trap, organizations need to go one step further. Create more contact moments, generate more possibilities to build your brand and offer more relevance to your customer than only your core products. Organizations need a platform to pull customers towards them: branded utilities are crucial.
A branded utility is a set of services, often digital, created by and linked to a brand. These services are all connected by a central theme that adds value to your customers and

Figure 2.3 Branded utilities

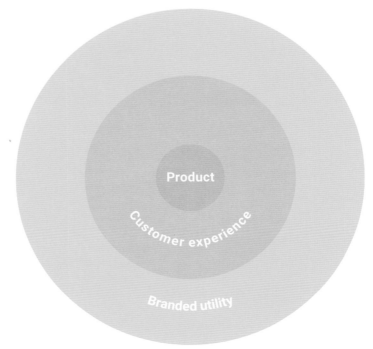

supports them to make their life easier. Via the added value of these services the customer feels more connected to your brand. The services are not directly linked to your core customer journey, though they are closely related to it. The services don't improve the customer journey, but can lead to more extended or even completely new journeys and new business models to give a broader relevance to your brand and thus create more contacts with your customers.

In this context, a lot of energy organizations have developed their own smart thermostats. With these thermostats and the accompanying app, customers have frequent and relevant contacts with the energy company instead of only the monthly or even yearly invoice. Some energy companies started to use the thermostats as gifts to loyal customers or as welcome presents to attract new customers. Nowadays however, customers from rival companies can also buy them and experience the benefits this company has to offer to them.

This is a good service, however it is not yet a branded utility. It is a standalone service. Only when the services are completely part of the total experience do we call it a branded utility. That means, in the case of the energy companies, that the data from the smart thermostats should be incorporated in their databases and used within the journey whenever relevant. The smart thermostat and other services provided by the energy companies should be a comprehensive journey.

A good example is Nutricia, who created tools that are relevant for the complete customer journey ('being a mother') and in this way adds more value to their core product: baby nutrition. You can find more information on this case on page 56. Another good example is Nike, which created the branded utility Nike+: an app to track your running performance and let you share it with others. With this service, Nike appropriates the 'running theme' by going beyond only offering running gear.

Benefits of a good branded utility:

- **Strengthens the brand power:** a utility claims unique authority in the broader context of the product. For example, Nike claiming the 'Running' theme. This way, Nike creates more contact moments to build the brand than would ever be possible by solely selling the running gear.
- **Improves loyalty:** more relevant contacts strengthen the customer relation. The user of Nike+ experiences positive contacts and the unique added value of Nike more often.
- **Leads to possible new revenue streams:** a good branded utility provides so much added value that users should be willing to pay for it. We mentioned the smart thermostats earlier. They lead to whole new revenue streams for energy companies today.
- **Enriches customer profiles:** the frequent interactions via the branded utility lead to a more complete view on customers, since more data (about behavior, characteristics and preferences) becomes available. Nike learns a great deal from the users of the Nike+ app and so continuously improves their products and services.

And these benefits strengthen each other. The branded utility is a self-improving system: because of extra interactions, you obtain more customer data and thus more customer insights. Based on these insights, you can develop better propositions with a shorter time to market, so increased efficiency on product development and lower marketing costs. This leads to more added value for your customers, who will purchase more of your products and services. This leads again to more interactions, so more insights and so on. The longer this system works, the more intelligent it will become. You create a lock-in for your customers.

Design principles: setting clear guidelines for each experience

Within a company, different departments and different people work on the customer experience: product management, online marketing, operations, IT, account management, etc. All of them are directly or indirectly responsible for what the customer experiences.

How do you make sure that all these people are working towards the same goal? By defining clear design principles!
Design principles describe the experience you want to deliver to your customers. They function as guidance and framework for all customers, all customer journeys and all your company's products. They are generic enough to be applicable to all contacts, yet are concrete enough to ensure the right customer experience. No contact should conflict with design principles. As an illustration: a design principle 'we want to create distinctive experiences' is too generic, since it doesn't give guidance on how you want to distinguish yourself.
On the other side, a design principle of the type 'we surprise the customer right after the application' isn't good since it is only applicable to the buying phase.
Only when all employees take the design principles into account and live up to them will the customer truly feel the experience you want to deliver.

We already stated that valuable experiences should be RICH:
- **R**eflecting the brand values.
- **I**ndividualizing the experience.
- **C**ontributing to the business objectives.
- **H**armonizing the customer journey as a whole.

When defining the design principles, we therefore take four factors into account:

1 *The desired customer experience*
The desired customer experience should reflect your brand values. So not surprisingly, brand values are key input for the design principles. The design principles make the brand values concrete and open to one interpretation only. The brand value 'simplicity' could, for example, lead to a design principle 'the customer can do business with us quickly'. But it could also lead to 'the customer always understands what they need to do and what the next steps are'. The design principles should define the desired customer experience: how should your brand values be experienced by the customer? What kind of emotion should the customer have whenever and however having contact with your company?

2 Employee behavior

The design principles should also lead to clear guidance for all employees on what and what not to do. What do we expect from employees (either employees with or without direct customer contacts) in order to deliver the desired customer experience?

These design principles could be externally focused. For example, the Dutch, mainly online, retailer Cool Blue has as its motto 'Everything for a smile'. That means all employees should think that whatever they are doing will lead to a smile on a customer's face.

To create branded individual moments, employees need to be more empowered to ignore standard processes if circumstances require it. They need to be able to act in the best interest of the customer at that moment. A design principle such as 'we listen to our customers and do what is best for them' could therefore be helpful in order to create individual, yet consistent customer experiences.

The desire to create individual experiences may also lead to a more internally focused principle, e.g. regarding which data we need to capture and how. 'We always ask for a little bit of extra information from the customer to personalize the experience the next time' is an example of an internally focused design principle.

3 The contribution to the business objectives

CEX only sells if the desired experience is in line with your business objectives.

Therefore, in the design principles, the business objectives each contact should contribute to are made clear. If your objective is to lower costs, you might want to establish a principle like the following: at every contact, we appeal to the customer to make use of the online channels. But if your objective is to cross-sell, this principle does not lead to the desired experience.

A better design principle could then be 'at every contact we offer the customer another relevant product'.

The latter immediately addresses an important starting point for using design principles: there might be some contact moments where you cannot live up to all your design principles.

Imagine that a customer contacts you to complain about one of your services. Do you really want to offer this customer another relevant product at that moment?

For every situation, you need to think about how you can match the design principles. If this is not possible or not logical, you don't have to match all the principles. However, the experience may never conflict with a single one of the principles!

4 The use of contact channels

No single customer contact stands on its own. Customers have different contacts during different moments via different channels. Since the total customer experience is the sum of all these contacts, consistency is key. The main purpose of the design principles is to ensure this consistency, regardless of the type of contact, and regardless of the contact channel.

To harmonize the customer journey as a whole, we need to ensure all channels are perfectly aligned. Therefore, the fourth angle from which to define design principles is the use of contact channels.

In line with the company's strategy, a company might have a clear preference for the use of a certain channel. With the design principles, we can ensure the company's preferred channel is taken into account. The customer journey can then be designed in such a way that this preferred channel is also the best and most logical option for the customer. A frequently used design principle to illustrate this is 'mobile first'. All experiences are designed to optimize the customer journey via the mobile channel. This leads to completely different experiences to a design principle such as 'the customer can choose whatever channel they prefer. All channels are open'.

Whatever the design principle regarding the contact channels might be, in the end the customer will always choose their own favorite channel. So even with a design principle such as 'mobile first', this doesn't mean all other channels can be neglected.

How to define the design principles

Of course, the customer is the main starting point, so customer insights are crucial to define the design principles. But we can't emphasize enough that a good customer experience is both beneficial for the customer and for your company. Therefore, the strategy, vision and mission of your company are also important sources for the design principles.

Next to customer insights and business insights, market insights need to be taken into account. Trends in the market, technological developments and competitors' behavior can all lead to refinements on design principles.

To offer a consistent customer experience to the customer, it is essential that all employees agree to the design principles. Defining them is a joint effort of Marketing, Sales, Communication, Customer Services, but also of internal departments such as IT and Operations. As you can imagine, this will lead to a lot of discussions, which is good! But be mindful that this doesn't lead to concessions and therefore to mediocre design principles. By using words such as 'always', 'never', 'everybody', 'everywhere', the principles are more powerful, but the discussions are fiercer as well. It is better to discuss a little bit longer than to agree on overly non-specific design principles. You will probably end up in the same discussions later on, or translate the design principles in different ways, which might ultimately result in inconsistency in the experience.

Key take-aways:

- Improving your customer experience is not only about process optimization, it is about creating real relations with your customers.
- Your brand is your most important asset to create distinctive experiences. If your brand values are not distinctive, your customer experience won't ever be either. Think of emotional values next to functional values.
- Although all experiences should be in line with your brand values, it is important to define moments where your brand really makes a difference: brand moments.
- Individual moments should be RICH: Reflecting the brand values, Individualizing the experience, Contributing to the business objectives, Harmonizing the customer journey as a whole.
- Use your brand values to define your branded utilities: new services linked to your brand and adding further value to the customer.
- In order to ensure all experiences are synchronized, clear design principles are key.

M&M's

Adding character to a candy

Everyone knows the little colorful chocolates from the Mars company, with the letter 'M' imprinted on them. The first M&M's were products in 1941. The original candy was a 'plain' M&M's, with a milk chocolate filling. Nowadays the M&M's product range has been expanded towards a wide variety of sizes, types of chocolate, types of nut and other fillings. For special occasions, such as Christmas, limited editions are added to this collection. Every day, about 400 million M&M's are produced worldwide.

M&M's created characters to add emotion to the chocolate

Frank C. Mars, founder of the Mars Company, came up with the idea for M&M's when he saw British soldiers eating Smarties in the 1930s. Because of the candy-coating, the chocolate would not melt and this made it possible for soldiers to carry chocolate with them. The M&M's slogan "Melts in your mouth, not in your hand" refers to that. Over the years, new variations of M&M's were introduced. However, this could not prevent them from becoming a regular candy. In order to build a real brand, M&M's had to change something.

Since fun is an important brand value for M&M's, they created characters representing the candies and used them in their marketing activities. The computer-animated illustrations added a personal touch to the candies and helped M&M's to stand out again. It helped them to evoke so-called 'anthropomorphism': consumers attribute human traits, emotions and intentions to impersonal products. Most campaigns feature the dominant, sarcastic Red, who is very confident and thinks he knows it all, and the cheerful, but naive Yellow, Red's best friend. Red represents the original M&M's, while Yellow the peanut type. Blue, Green, Orange and Ms Brown, the Chief Chocolate Officer, complete the team nowadays. These six characters add emotions to the candies and have created true brand fans for M&M's, which are not just a candy, but also a strong brand.

Experience stores and online presence create a unique M&M's world

To add even more experience to the chocolates, M&M's opened experience stores in top locations in Las Vegas, Orlando, New York, London (the largest candy store in the world) and Shanghai: M&M's World. In the shops, visitors can meet the characters in person. The shops are full of M&M's merchandise, ranging from dishware and pens to bikinis and watches. It truly is a world of its own.

Of course, alongside all the merchandise, you can buy M&M's in the shops. Giant walls with M&M's sorted by color give you the opportunity to buy your favorite candy in your favorite color.

Besides M&M's World, the website also plays an important role in branding M&M's. The colorful site lists the different products, introduces the characters and links to the different M&M's shops. Obviously, merchandise from M&M's world can be bought here, but there is also a link to MYM&M's, giving the visitor the opportunity to personalize their M&M's. Here, you can choose your favorite colors, select a text or even a picture to imprint on the M&M's, and choose your own package to create your own personal M&M's. Creating your own personalized M&M's has raised brand awareness and has increased sales.

M&M's keeps on innovating

And still the M&M's experience continues to grow. M&M's keeps on creating funny, innovative branding activities to entice customers to become brand fans. One example: last year, in line with the US elections, M&M's organized their own election. People could try three possible new flavors and vote for the one they liked best. One of the outcomes is that M&M's has now added a coffee flavored M&M's to its product range.

What your company can learn from M&M's:

- Always act from your brand values. For M&M's the core brand value is fun and this is powered both functionally and emotionally.
- Create a personal bond between your customers and your products by humanizing your products. This might be a character like those M&M's created, but giving your products names of a person or naming your chatbot has a similar effect.
- Add character to your products and let that be reflected in all your customer interactions. How do you want your customers to perceive your brand and/or products?
- Think of new ways to be present in your customer's life, next to your primary role. New customer contacts increase the possibility to create a true relationship.
- Keep on innovating to stay ahead of the competition.

NUTRICIA

Data usage to build and nurture the customer relationship

Nutricia, part of the Danone group, specializes in early life nutrition and advanced medical nutrition. Nutricia believes that by helping mums and babies get the right nutrition from the start of pregnancy until the baby is two years old, they can and will positively influence their short- and long-term health outcomes. Nutricia's Early Life Nutrition's priorities are to support mothers and babies to get the right nutrition in the first 1,000 days. They are introducing nutritious products, education and services for pregnant and breastfeeding women in an increasing number of global markets.

Nutricia created a 'pull platform' to support the complete 'mother journey'

Nutricia wants a close relation with mothers and future mothers. They focus on women who want to get pregnant to their child's first two years. In order to build relationships with these mothers, Nutricia has developed a platform that supports them in all kinds of ways. Nutricia offers useful and relevant information, at any step in the mother journey. In this way, a true pull platform is created: a platform so relevant for the mother that it is consistently attracting mothers to go there.

The platform is currently being piloted in the Netherlands. Since results are far beyond expectations, the platform will soon be rolled out to other countries as well.

To make the platform as relevant as possible, Nutricia identified the emotions mothers have during the journey and the moments of truth. Based on these insights, Nutricia is able to add value to mothers by supporting them with general help, support and information each step of the way.

Though sales is ultimately an important objective for Nutricia, they have chosen not to try to convert the mothers directly, but first to build a close relationship with them. And like every relationship, this starts with getting to know each other. Nutricia asked the mother the current situation (becoming pregnant, pregnant, baby or toddler) and, if relevant, the due date or date of birth. Based on this information, the conversation starts. The platform offers useful content for each stage, for example explanations of what's happening to your baby at a given moment, nutrition advice from experts, tools to support your motherhood and practical tips.

A consistent omnichannel experience supports the total mother journey

The 'mother journey' program goes beyond the online platform however. It offers a complete omnichannel experience. Some examples:

Nutricia developed a mobile app (their branded utility) where mothers can find all information regarding the pregnancy and newborn baby. Moreover, the new mother can save information and pictures of her baby and herself in the app. She can easily share them with friends and family. Convenient tools help to remind her when to feed the baby, also if a partner or babysitter is taking care of the baby. And from the app, the mothers can easily go to the other elements of the program.

Nutricia ensures it is present in all online places where mothers gather information and discuss matters with each other. Nutricia is also present in the relevant offline places, for example at the Nine Months Fair, a fair in Amsterdam where pregnant women can find all information and products needed to take care of their baby. Nutricia offers them a convenient service: all products they buy at the fair are delivered straight to their homes. By using the online shop to register the orders, Nutricia ensures this data is collected at the same central database. Another example are the kiosks at strategic places , for example the Central Station of Amsterdam. By registering via an online form on the screen of the kiosk, the mothers (or fathers) can easily purchase Nutricia products.

Data is the core of the whole nutrition experience

In all these places, Nutricia collects a lot of data and insights from the mothers. All these various data sources are consolidated in one database, ensuring enormously rich profiles that are subject to constant growth via multichannel enrichment and mining. With these, Nutricia is able to provide tailor-made services to every parent with the right content, services and tools, and personal advice and offerings precisely in line with, for example, the exact age and health situation of the child. Nutricia uses this data to build and nurture relationships. Months in advance of the birth, Nutricia takes its time to identify the mother or future mother's problem and the hurdles that she experiences in solving that problem. Nutricia educates them if necessary, carefully selecting the information and tools that would be helpful. The frequent contacts provide all kinds of possibilities to establish a connection. The result is that by the time the mother is ready to purchase, Nutricia's products are a natural given. The results of the platform exceed expectations by far on 'brand of first choice', NPS, and the rate of interaction with the brand. The program has reached growth of about 75% each month and average monthly rebuy growth of 140%.

What your company can learn from Nutricia:

- Make customer data key to build relevant and personal experiences. Use this data as a starting point for everything you do.
- Give relevant content to your customers so they want to use your services, provide you with even more data which allows you to become even more relevant etc.
- Ensure all your services are linked to each other so data is centrally stored.
- Take time to build relations, to be patient, and not start selling too quickly or – even worse – straightaway.
- Select a clear domain you want to be active in and build in that domain a pull platform to attract your customers.

PORSCHE

Building relationships by addressing emotions

Porsche, officially Porsche AG, is the German luxury automobile manufacturer well-known for its high-performance sports cars. Ever since the first Porsche was created in 1947, the company has been continuously striving to create the perfect sports car. The underlying Porsche Principle is simple: always get the most out of everything. After sports cars, Porsche also produces high-end fashion articles like watches, pens and trolleys with the Porsche Design brand.

Porsche adds emotion to every touchpoint in the journey to build relationships

Porsche positions itself as an emotional brand. They do not only want to be a sports car but want to be a daily emotion. Customers don't just buy a Porsche to get from one place to another, but because they enjoy the experience of driving and really care about their car. An important ingredient of Porsche's success has therefore been its long-term relationship with its customers. If you have dreamt of a Porsche for a long time and you are going to spend more than 100,000 euro on a vehicle, you're more than likely to expect an extremely high quality of service.
This means the customer must not only have a memorable buying experience, but should have the same feeling while owning the car. The entire end-to-end journey is therefore constantly measured and shared with everyone within Porsche.

One of the results is that Porsche found out that repair is an important touchpoint for the customer. Repairing your Porsche is not purely functional but it is also emotional: something you really like needs to be fixed. Trusting that your car is well taken care of is important. Therefore, Porsche is always looking to add more emotion to a functional repair. One concrete example is that the mechanic makes a personal movie-clip when your car is checked. He addresses you personally, quickly introduces himself and explains the points of attention. The movie is shared via a personal e-mail, so the owner can take a look at their convenience and decide what they want repaired and what not. After the e-mail the customer is called to discuss the points of attention and to discuss what the mechanic will or won't repair.

Another example of the personal, relationship-building activities are the exclusive events Porsche drivers get invited to, such as major car events or smaller events at local dealers. There is also a Porsche club, not owned by Porsche, but it retains a strong partnership with the club.

Shaping the future by blending history and innovation

The automotive industry is in the middle of a massive technological revolution. It needs to look for new ways to serve its customers. E-mail and video are examples of this, but the technology is clearly not only restricted to the services. It also enables companies like Porsche to rethink their business models. Porsche set itself the strategy to shape the future of the sports car. A future that will blend the history and values of Porsche with innovative technologies. Topics like digitization and connectivity are important for Porsche to implement its strategy. As one of the first initiatives, Porsche introduced a concept: 'Share a Porsche'.

'Share a Porsche' makes it possible for a broader target audience to live their dream to drive a Porsche. They do not really own it, but lease it and share the Porsche within a group of up to four people. Together they agree on the kind of Porsche they want to drive, the amount of mileage they expect to travel and how long they want to share it. These factors will then be used to estimate a fixed monthly rate. Porsche places a telematic tool in the car, which is connected with the mobile network and collects data. By using the 'Share a Porsche' app the members of the group can see the availability and make reservations for specific days they want to drive the Porsche. The data collected is shown in the app and prevents possible disputes between the different owners by clearly visualizing and showing the usages per driver. With these new technologies, Porsche makes driving an exclusive sports car one step closer to a broader audience and is able to attract more customers with their products and services.

What your company can learn from Porsche:

- Think not only about how you can improve the customer experience functionally, but also take the emotional aspects into account.
- Think about the customer experience from an end-to-end perspective.
- Make ordinary events such as repair personal and special to create an unexpected and satisfactory feeling.
- Use technical possibilities to enrich your experience or even use it to reinvent the accessibility of your product.

BRUSSELS AIRLINES

'Belgitude' ambassador

Brussels Airlines is Belgium's largest airline and operates around 300 flights to over 90 destinations in Europe, Africa, North America and India daily. Brussels Airlines is a member of the Lufthansa Group and Star Alliance. The airline is based at Zaventem Brussels Airport and the total number of passengers has grown over the last years to almost 8 million. Brussels Airlines strives to be the most personal airline, bringing people together and making traveling pleasant again.

Brussels Airlines treats its 'guests' with 'belgitude'

Just like many traditional airlines, Brussels Airlines also faces strong competition from low-cost carriers. In a short time period, European low-cost airlines Vueling, Easyjet and Ryanair all started operations at Brussels Airport, the home base of Brussels Airlines. Although these three newcomers are all strongly competing on price, Brussels Airlines understood they had to define a different strategy. Of course, prices should be competitive, but Brussels Airlines added a distinctive customer experience to that. They wanted to get out of the commodity trap by becoming the most personal airline. The airline doesn't see their customers as passengers, but as guests. Which makes the job of the company not to just take people from one place to another, but to bring people together.

Brussels Airlines strives to make traveling as pleasant as possible by going the extra mile: adding a personal touch, positively surprising their customers and adding a further Belgian touch. This Belgian touch in particular is what Brussels Airlines tries to express as clearly as possible. They strive to be an ambassador of so-called 'belgitude', a word used to express the Belgian soul and identity, synonymous of 'joie de vivre' or enjoyment.

Having been occupied by many foreign European powers throughout history, and given the fact that most Belgians either consider themselves Flemish, Walloon or part of Brussels, belgitude is important to the country. And Brussels Airlines wants to build on this belgitude by constantly promoting the uniqueness of Belgium.

Flight attendants wear Belgian designed fashion and serve special Belgian beers, Belgian wines and Belgian chocolates, Belgian Michelin-star chefs prepare the on-board food, and Belgian products can be bought tax-free during the flight. But Brussels Airlines goes beyond even that. They also decided to promote this belgitude via the aircraft.

'We fly you to the home of Tintin'

Brussels Airlines created a unique Tintin aircraft: an Airbus A320 inspired by the Tintin comics. The Belgian character Tintin is like a symbol of all the good things that come from Belgium. And since Tintin flies around the world on his adventures and meets a lot of different people, Tintin perfectly fits the airline's mission. The whole airplane looks like a giant shark, based on the submarine of Professor Calculus in the cartoons. On the fuselage, it says: 'We fly you to the home of Tintin'. As well as the outside, the interior of the plane is also in Tintin style and the comic with the shark submarine in it can of course be bought on board the aircraft.

To celebrate the partnership with the Red Devils (the Belgian soccer team) and the Belgian Soccer Association, another airplane was dedicated to the Red Devils. Trident, as the plane is baptized, is all red, with the colors of the Belgian Flag and a prominent trident. And both the outside and the inside of the aircraft are decorated with the Belgian Red Devils players, their coaches and Belgian soccer fans. Brussels Airlines sees the partnership with the Red Devils as a perfect match, since they both bring people together and are proud to be Belgian.

A third aircraft was painted in honor of the Belgian surrealist painter René Magritte. Magritte is renowned for looking at things from a different angle, just like Brussels Airlines does.

Brussels Airlines can't beat its competition solely in the air

Alongside completely making over airplanes, Brussels Airlines is also looking for easier ways to connect to Belgian icons. The Smurfs are a famous worldwide brand, yet few people know they are Belgian. As part of their ambition to promote belgitude as well as their continuous efforts to make traveling with children as pleasant as possible, Brussels Airlines brought them on board. Children who fly long-haul now get a Smurf lunchbox with coloring books, memory games and finger puppets. New smurfs such as Safari Smurf have been created specially for the airline, all in order to create new touchpoints with guests.

Brussels Airlines understands it can't beat its competition solely in the air. Therefore, next to changing airplanes and the onboard experience, the company redesigned other moments of truth in the flying journey as well.
Brussels Airlines for example redesigned the booking journey together with their guests to create a clear and simple booking experience. This led to an impressive 42% improved conversion rate on the website.
Their business lounge at Brussels Airport was also completely redesigned, combining comfort, technology, design and again the Belgian touch, both via food and beverages as well as via inspiration from the rich history of the country.

What your company can learn from Brussels Airlines:

- Be authentic, choose where you want to stand out based on what is important to you and to your customers.
- Once you've picked a direction in which to stand out, see whether you can translate this into as many touchpoints as possible. And create your own new touchpoints as well.
- Depending on your industry, brand values can make you distinctive, but this could also be something more fundamental, such as your heritage.
- Think about the complete customer journey from a customer's point of view and find areas to improve.

TONY'S CHOCOLONELY

Clear purpose helps customers' involvement with your brand

Tony's Chocolonely (Tony's) is a Dutch chocolate brand, known for its ambition to make the global chocolate chain 100% slave free. Since 2012, Tony's has been buying cocoa beans directly from farmer cooperatives in Ivory Coast and Ghana. They have proven in the last 10 years that they can be a 'good company' while making money. They have built a very successful and financially self-sufficient business in the Netherlands by using their own value-chain.

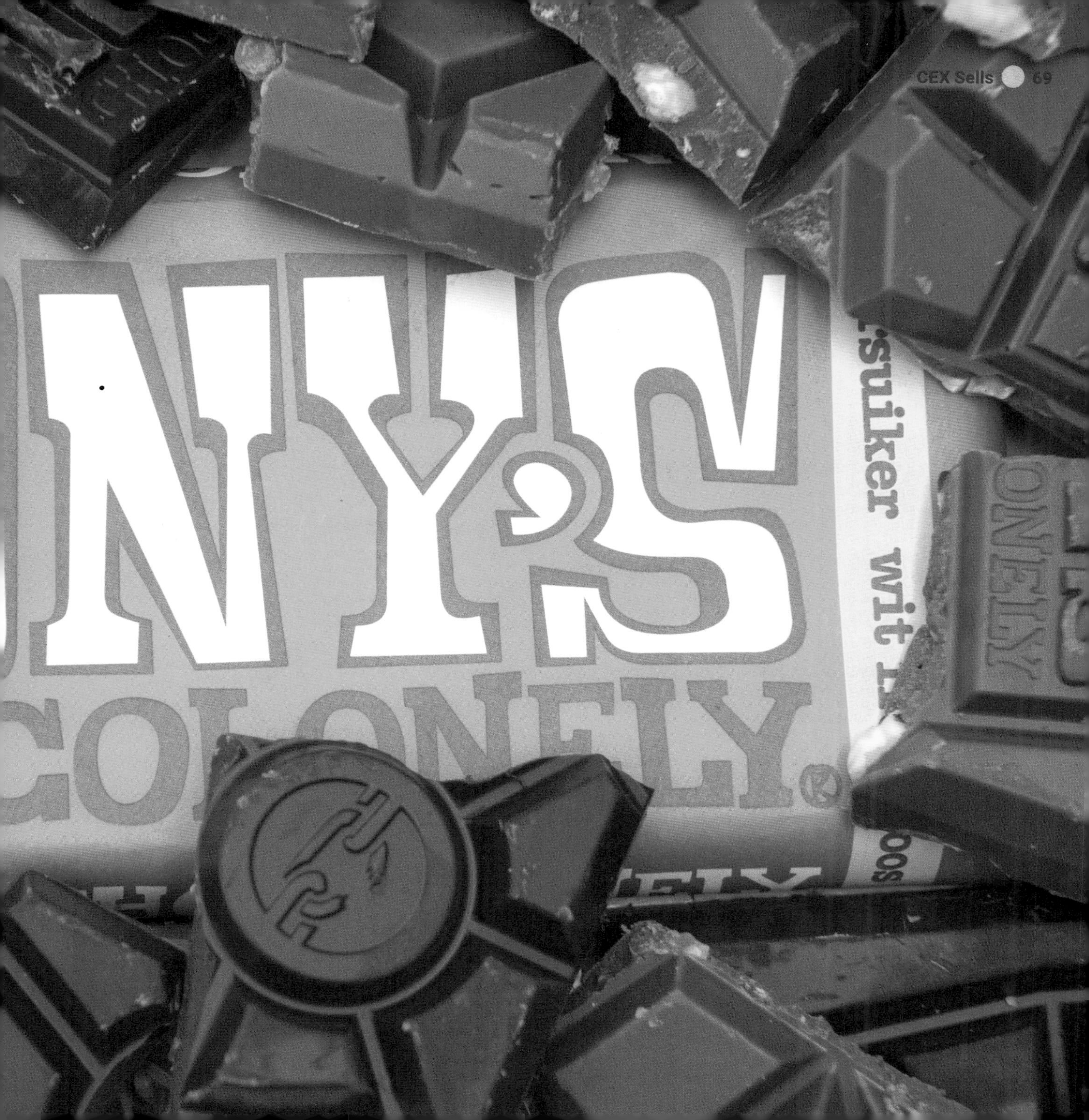
NY'S
COLONELY
suiker wit

Create customer involvement with a clear mission

In 2003 the Dutch investigative reporter Teun van de Keuken was shocked to discover that most of the cocoa was still harvested by slaves and - even worse – by child slaves. He investigated the use of slavery within the cocoa industry and wanted to do something about it. He decided to roll up his sleeves himself and ate a couple of chocolate bars. After which he turned himself in to the authorities as a chocolate criminal. By eating chocolate, he was complicit in slavery. But the public prosecutor wouldn't prosecute him. Teun didn't give up and went looking for witnesses; victims of chocolate consumption. He found four boys who had worked as slaves on a cocoa farm in Ivory Coast. They provided evidence against Teun and the 2,136 other chocolate consumers who in the meantime had joined Teun in his stride. On November 29th 2005, still awaiting the judge's decision, Teun (Tony) decided to lead by example and make slave-free (lonely) chocolate (choco) bars himself. Tony has a clear mission *"100% slave free chocolate. Not just their chocolate, but all chocolate worldwide"*. This mission is so strong, Tony started with this purpose and only then started the business.

Help the customer in understanding the purpose

Tony's goes further than producing and selling a chocolate bar, they play an important role in exposing international abuses in the chocolate industry. They create awareness for the problem and lead by example by making 'slave free chocolate' themselves. The company uses real stories to be credible. They let themselves be prosecuted and found four boys working in slavery. But they do not only tell stories, and also show the customer what they can do about it. Customers can buy a product to help and join the mission; the chocolate bar, not a very expensive and boring tasting piece of candy but an interesting, well-priced bar which can be found in popcorn/disco dip and orange/rosemary flavors. Tony's 'action perspective' combines their mission with possible action which does change the world. It results not in an altruistic behavior supporting the

mission but a consumer that enjoys the product as well as being able to do something towards their shared goal. The chocolate bar itself is different to other chocolate brands. The bars are divided unequal pieces that resemble western Africa. This makes visible the wrong and unequal division of wealth in the chocolate value chain. Not only a vehicle for the brand story but also for creating awareness, again and again. Consumers remember the product through the unequal pieces that are not that easy to break and even leave pieces of chocolate on your couch. Customers tell this story to others and the purpose of Tony is shared and remembered. Another example is the roadmap that is printed on the packaging of the bar. This wrap clearly shows what they have done and are doing towards their goal. Tony's let their customer enjoy the product and at the same time understand the reality.

Be authentic and therefore a trusting partner

It sounds a cliché but being authentic is crucial. It is not about transparency, the amount you share and how accessible certain information is. It is about the truth of your words. Tony's are striving for a fair share in the chocolate value chain but are aware this cannot be done in a year or so. They are open about their journey and openly explain why some parts of the bars are not 100% slave free yet. Tony's also have a broader target setting with impact analyses.

An independent firm analyses them every year and they use this impact matrix as a target alongside financial parameters. In their annual FAIR report (instead of an annual report) they researched what they heard on social media, from customers, journalists and cocoa farmers in West Africa. Their conclusions were input for the report.

They also communicated about what did not work and what they did not do. They are striving for a fair share in the chocolate value chain and therefor using "fair" in all their communication. Every year they have their aniFAIRsary where they publish their annual Fair report.

What your company can learn from Tony Chocolonely:

- Tell a powerful authentic story.
- Help customers to understand your mission and make them feel part of it.
- Give the customer an 'action perspective', by showing them what they can do.
- Prove your value in the customer's life not only as a customer but as a human.
- Translate your story into the whole customer journey. Not only in the product, but also in other touchpoints such as an 'aniFAIRsary'.

GENERAL ELECTRIC

A 125-year-old startup

General Electric, often abbreviated to GE, is an American multinational technology-, electronics,- and services concern. Or, as they put it themselves: they 'create things that build, move, power and cure our world.' Ever since Thomas Edison founded the company, they strive to make our world work better. GE is made up of six segments to do this:
Power & Water, Oil and Gas, Aviation, Healthcare, Transportation and Capital. GE is one of the biggest companies in the world, with businesses in over 180 countries.

GE

GE Watthour Meter

KILOWATTHOURS

138/9

240 v 3 w FM

Customer focus in a product-oriented B2B world through strong cultural beliefs

GE-founder Edison himself created the mindset that GE should make the world work better. Starting with the light bulb, Edison developed this idea into the first electricity grid, bringing electricity to the world. Continuously improving the products was the main focus for GE for a long time, and still is.

However, in today's B2B world, customer orientation is increasingly important, but getting customer experience into your company's DNA is hard if, for over a century, your focus has been product innovation and technology.

GE wants to be a digital industrial company: not purely digital, not purely industrial, but truly hybrid. GE expresses the new and vital connections among machines, data, and people for the current era. It is transforming the world by creating connected machines so they are faster, safer and more effective. How should that be reflected in the customer experience?

Though in existence for over 125 years now, GE still sees itself as a startup. A 125-year-old startup. GE is always experimenting to disrupt the status quo, even though this status quo is often created by GE itself. The cultural beliefs of GE express this as follows:
- Customers determine our success.
- Stay lean to go fast.
- Learn and adapt to win.
- Empower and inspire each other.
- Deliver results in an uncertain world.

All this is summed up in the current tagline: 'imagination at work', highlighting people inventing and making substantial contributions in scientific research, manufacturing and technology.

GE uses many online moments to share the GE story

To share this with the world, the internet is important to GE. It sees the internet changing from a mainly consumer focused internet to an industrial focused internet. The internet helps GE to make the big, impersonal work GE is doing feel personal and close to the consumer.

Social media plays an important role in this. Since innovation and being the first is part of GE's DNA, the company is often an early adopter of new platforms. Employees of GE are early adopters themselves and they get the freedom to experiment (or, as they call it, 'the freedom to fail'). Being active on, amongst others, Instagram, Twitter, Facebook, Snapchat, Vine and Periscope, GE even outperforms many B2C companies. All this branded content is clearly targeted to people interested in innovation and discovery.

Together with social media, GE has its own content platform: GE Reports. This platform covers GE's transformation into the world's largest digital industrial company by sharing news, videos and social media posts. New content is added daily on the use of software and data to connect, control and improve machines and entire industries. This content is largely created by employees of GE, but also external views are shared. The whole website is not a company blog, but a true online magazine focusing on storytelling. The stories address real problems and innovative technologies to solve them, and they are sometimes so popular that they get picked up by other media such as 'The Washington Post' and even outside the US. These successes inspire employees within GE to share what they are working on via GE Reports. A daily e-mail notifies the reader to the new content on the website, and of course these stories are also shared via all the social media.

Elaborate content strategy to attract potential buyers, investors and employees

The internet is not the only place for GE to connect to its audience, however. TV remains an important medium, although it's getting ever harder to get the viewers' attention. GE therefore created, together with National Geographic, a series called 'Breakthrough, showing how cutting-edge innovations pushing the boundaries of science will change our lives'. The first series was praised by critics and a second one is due out shortly.

The innovative story of GE is important to set the right image for buyers of their products. Having all these additional contacts with this audience gives GE the opportunity to clearly show its brand identity. On average, visitors of GE reports stay almost four minutes on the site, so GE is making a genuine connection with the audience. Next to buyers and potential buyers, the content strategy also attracts potential investors and employees. Now GE has way more touchpoints to connect to all these target groups and feed their shared enthusiasm about science.

What your company can learn from GE:

- Define clear cultural beliefs that express the kind of company you want to be and share these company-wide.
- Ensure your cultural beliefs support the best results for the customer: values such as 'lean', 'empower' and 'inspire' could be advantageous.
- Add additional touchpoints to create true relationships with your (potential) customers.
- Define the company story you want to share and tell this story consistently across all channels.
- Use clever facts about your company, for instance the inspiring founder, to set yourself truly apart from competitors.
- Use all possible media to share your story with your target audience.
- Create your own content to attract your target audience.

Chapter **3**

THE CUSTOMER JOURNEY DOES NOT EXIST

HOW DATA IS NEEDED TO CREATE TAILOR-MADE CUSTOMER JOURNEYS

The customer journey is the sum of all customer contacts. To manage these contacts a lot of organizations therefore define the customer journey for the products or services they offer. But this implies all customers have the same contacts in the same order via the same channels. Of course, this is not the reality. In practice, each customer defines their own customer journey, so there is a vast number of customer journeys. How do you ensure each customer gets the best customer journey for their personal situation? And how do you still keep it manageable? In order to do so, data is key. While we have discussed the use of customer journey data to measure the customer journey in the previous chapter, we'll now discuss the use of customer data to give each customer a tailor-made experience.

Don't think of journeys, think of combinations of touchpoints

The word 'journey' suggests a linear sequence of customer contacts. A journey has a beginning, a middle and an end. This might have been true in the past, especially for journeys within one channel. But nowadays the exponential growth of channels on which the customer can interact with organizations has led to a situation where customers define their own 'omni-channel' journey, and that journey is far more complicated to grasp. Customers don't systematically look for information, make decisions, use your products, ask for advice etc. They go back and forth in their journey and some contact moments don't happen once, but repetitively.

Organizations must make a continuous effort to be present on a multitude of channels, showing they understand today's customers and that they are looking beyond the paradigm of the 'customer journey'.

Process mining to optimize your journey

One commonly used way of understanding this non-linear customer journey is 'process mining'. Process mining is a combination of Data Mining and Business Process Management. It is a methodology that allows the reconstruction and visualization of the process based on logs from information systems. Specialized data-mining algorithms are applied to these logs to identify trends and patterns. This way the most common processes and thus the most common customer journeys are identified. This has two benefits:

1. Firstly, you can optimize the omni-channel experience by ensuring these routes are optimally supported by your (omni-channel) processes and systems. An example to illustrate this: if process mining shows that a lot of your customers first look for an answer on your website and then try to reach the contact center, you can optimize the contact center by improving the level of knowledge there and ensuring more information can be given by phone.

2. Secondly, knowing the paths within the journey helps you to simplify the customer journey for your customer. In our previous example, you might want to change the content on the website to make sure the customers can find the answer online and don't need to reach your contact center at all. Process mining is not only about optimizing the steps in the customer journey, but it is also about removing unnecessary steps and simplifying the journey for the customer. It shows you the steps the customer made previously in a contact moment and thus helps you to analyze the root causes of contact moments.

However, even with process mining, you can never be one hundred percent sure of the journey a specific customer will make. Therefore, organizations should try to apply uniform customer processes and content as much as possible. Independent from the channel a customer chooses, the customer must follow the same steps with the same information. This enables the customer to go from one channel to another, without feeling lost on their journey.

Aiming for the 360° customer perspective for data-driven customer journeys

So each customer defines their own customer journey and thus each individual customer experience. How do we make sure each customer gets the right experience?
To achieve this, data is key. We already discussed that you need data on a customer level regarding the contact moments to be able to perform process mining and find out what type of customer journeys exist. Ideally, however, you do not only know what contact moments the customer has, but you know far more about this customer. Companies strive to a '360-degree customer view' as we call it (see page 81).

We mentioned that the growth of contact channels with which customers can interact with companies has meant the end of the linear customer journey. On the other hand, the growth of digital and mobile contact channels has caused an increase in the number of interactions between a customer and organizations, leading to an explosion of customer data.
Within the 360° customer view, we distinguish nine types of data. For each type of data we see that more and more data is becoming available.
Based on all this data, organizations define different customer segments, optimize the customer journey (both for sales and services) and keep on optimizing it. Naturally, the more data available, the better. However, even with only limited data, organizations can already get a lot of valuable insights to make the customer journey relevant to each single target customer.

Redefining segmentation: data-driven personas

Hopefully, your company's corporate strategy states which customers it is that you want to focus on. It should state which customers are your target audience and for whom you want to create the best experiences. This might mean that some customers might not get the best experience. But that is no problem, as long as they are not part of your target audience. To illustrate this, if you are focusing on young people, you might want to make use of the latest technologies and use informal and 'hip' language. Older people might not understand the technologies, or like the language. They might want more traditional means of contact. But that's ok. They are not your target audience. If you try to meet their wishes too, you'll create a diffuse customer experience. You cannot create a consistent experience and will probably end up in the middle. As a result, young people will not see you so distinctively within the industry, but nor will the older people. Consequently, you won't really create a branded experience for either of them.
The smaller the target audience, the closer the similarities between customers and the easier it will be to create a compelling experience for all of them. But some organizations clearly state in their strategy that they want to focus on a broad target audience. For example, a car insurer might want to focus on all people having a car. In that case, segmentation helps you to create compelling experiences for all your target customers in the appropriate way.

Data driven segmentation to support your business objectives

In order not to overcomplicate things, organizations use segmentation models to cluster their customers in generic groups. Obviously, all customers within one group should be as homogeneous as possible, while the differences between the groups should be as significant as possible.
Since segmentation is never a goal on its own, but one that supports business objectives, the type of segmentation needed is highly dependent on the objectives. Sales-driven companies tent to segment based on customer value. This can either be the current value, for example, based on current product possession,

or future value, based on additional sales possibilities and lifetime. Let's take a bank as an example. They might differentiate between customers with only a bank account and customers with a mortgage.

However, these segments might have the same needs regarding the customer journey. Whether a customer has a bank account or a mortgage, they might have exactly the same customer journey when they are looking for a loan at the bank.

Next to value-based segmentation, there is need-based segmentation. Need-based segmentation means you are truly focusing on the different customer needs. Customer-centric organizations that strive towards high NPS, and thus utmost loyalty, most often use a need-based segmentation.

Criteria often used for need-based segmentation are demographic criteria, such as life stages; for our bank example, this means customers having their first child could be a different segment to retired people.

However, both the new parents and the retired people may have the same needs; maybe they both want to feel in control and want to know all the details of a product. Or maybe they don't care and just completely follow the advice from others.

As a result, solely value-based or solely need-based segmentation is never 100% correct. Therefore, more and more organizations want to include as much data as possible when defining their segments: this is data-driven segmentation.

Based on all data available, they create a prediction model to define which customers are most valuable for your company. 'Valuable' is of course then related to your business objectives: which high end customers are most likely to buy more, to give you high NPS scores, to stay loyal, etc. Analytics can help you to define the variables that distinguish one segment from another.

Personas bring the segments to life

A good and practical way of using the data driven segmentation is with the use of personas: a characterization of typical customers of your company. You describe this customer by giving them a name, an age, an address, a household and even a profession and hobbies. You describe the type of products they use, what they like and dislike and how long they have been a customer. You also describe their attitude towards your brand, your products and your industry in general. And you describe their basic 'psychographic needs', e.g. whether they are concerned with health, what kind of lifestyle they want, what they enjoy in their free time, their attitude towards work.

In this way, you reach such a clear description of a person that you could easily envision him or her when defining the customer journey. When defined correctly, a company should be able to work with only three or four personas in order to optimize the journeys for all their customers.

But be aware that a persona is a simplification of the reality. It helps you to design the optimal journey, but as stated before the actual journey of this persona might be different. Some examples:

- Your persona might be a millennial who is always online and prefers to chat when having contact with a company. But when this persona loses his debit card, he immediately calls you.
- Or your persona is very sporty and always takes the bike to get to the office. However, when the temperature is below -10C even this person decides to take the bus.
- Your persona loves to eat out in good restaurants; however, during the holiday season they are short on budget and settle for a snack bar.

The context and situation determines the actual behavior of a persona in real life. And thus the actual customer journey and the actual customer experience.

Nevertheless, thinking of personas and defining the ideal customer journey per persona is a good start for successful customer experiences.

Figure 3.1 The 360° customer view

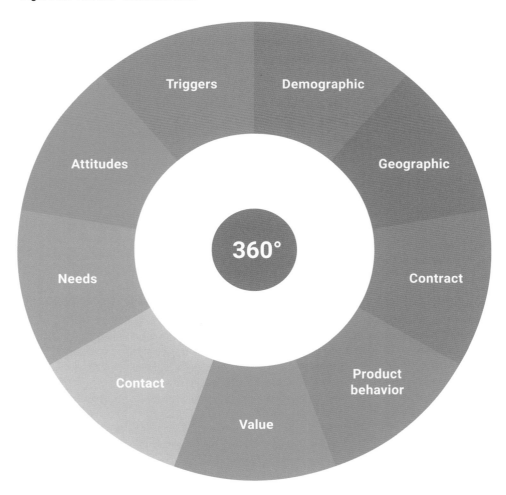

Demographic
Age, gender, education, income, profession, type of household, ...

Geographic
Mail address, invoice address, ...

Contract data
Product possession, product density, duration, migrations, payment plan, ...

Product behavior
Usage, claims, product changes, ...

Value
NPS, churn scores, lifetime, value, propensity scores, ...

Contact
Contact frequency, contact center logfiles, social media interactions, ...

Needs
Financial products, channel preferences, information need, value added services, ...

Attitudes
Risk-attitude, involvement, individual/social, intro/extravert, ...

Triggers
Offline, online, behavior, time, actions, life events, ...

Marketing automation to optimize efficiency in processes

Clever use of data in combination with digitization has made marketing processes, amongst other things, more efficient. One of the most common technologies used in this field is marketing automation: software that automates your marketing activities for you based on available data. Marketing technology is mainly used to generate more revenues. In our view, however, marketing technology is not so much about selling, but about strengthening the relationship with your customers and potential customers - which may lead to sales, but also to better service and more loyal customers. Marketing automation enables companies to send automated, yet personal e-mails to consumers based on their previous actions.

Let's say you run a hotel chain. To entice consumers to come to your hotels, you provide city guides via your website. Marketing automation can help you to convert consumers from just being interested in a city trip to sleeping at your hotel. How?

First of all, you let consumers leave their e-mail address when e.g. downloading the city guide from Amsterdam. Marketing automation technology lets you automatically send a 'thank you for downloading' email. A few days later, you send a follow up e-mail to all those people who downloaded the Amsterdam city guide. In this e-mail, you offer them a special deal when they book one or more nights at your hotel in Amsterdam.

In order to ensure the perfect follow-up, a notification is sent to the hotel in Amsterdam, so that they are fully aware of the deal just offered.

As you see, marketing automation allows you to target your customers in a personal way, based on the data provided by their own behavior. It enables you to encourage your customers to take the next steps, by providing them personal and relevant information or offers. As you can imagine, the more available data you have from your customers, the more personal and relevant the message can be.

Do keep in mind that marketing automation can help you to get new customers, but also to increase loyalty for your existing ones. By sending segmented, personal and therefore relevant information to your existing customers, this increases the relationship between these customers and your company. This will lead to more loyal customers who are more likely to purchase more from you. A sound content strategy is key to create the best content for those automated contacts.

Marketing automation changes the job of a marketer. Marketers still have to think about the right content for the right customer at the right time, but they have to be able to think in multiple 'flows' based on the 360-degree customer view. They have to create the ideal experience for each of these flows. Instead of one campaign, there are multiple ones running in parallel. This makes the job of a marketer more complex than in the past, but also far more effective.

Predictive analytics and machine learning for individual customer journeys

Smart usage of all available data is becoming key for deriving the most value from it. Not only in marketing campaigns as described above or in product development, but in all interactions throughout the whole customer journey.

Based on all available data, both within the company and data from external sources, organizations are able to create digital interactions that are personal and relevant. For organizations to create this competitive advantage throughout the customer journey, predictive analytics are vital.

To explain predictive analytics, we need to explain the difference between descriptive and predictive analytics. Automation used to be based on static business rules: if this... then that. To give you an example: if a customer buys car insurance online, we should show a pop-up offering a discount on travel insurance.

These business rules are based on what we call descriptive analytics, focusing on the 'rear view mirror'. Predictions are made based on an implicit assumption: what happened in the past will happen in the future in exactly the same way. For example: if a product is mainly bought by young women, we should mainly focus on young women in our campaign.

This is a prediction, it may even be a fact-based one, but as is often stated in the investment management industry, 'past performance is no guarantee of future results'.

With predictive analytics, we identify and address questions concerned with the future. We learn from our experience, take all kind of variables into account and predict future behavior in order to drive better decisions. Examples of predictive analytics are found in business, but also in sports, politics and social media. Facebook predicts which of 1,500 candidate posts (on average) will be most interesting to you and uses these predictions to personalize your newsfeed. Netflix sponsored a $1 million competition to better predict which movies you will like in order to continuously improve movie recommendations.

As you see in these examples, human experts can build models in order to predict future behavior. However, since the number of data sources, variables and models keep on growing, the question arises as to how to perform iterations on the created models in a more automated way: Machine Learning.

With Machine Learning we refer to the fact that computers have the ability to learn without being explicitly programmed by a human. Machines use 'past data' to find patterns that can be used to solve similar problems in the future. For example, a computer automatically uncovers the factors that are driving sales. Based on these factors, the machine performs different actions to different customers and each customer will get a personal journey, eventually optimizing sales results for the company. Machine learning helps you to navigate the overflow of data produced throughout the non-linear customer journey and leads to personal and relevant customer experiences.

Key take-aways:

- Customer journeys are non-linear. You need to standardize the different processes and contact in such a way that each customer can create their own journey.
- Use process mining to understand the most common customer journeys and to identify what to optimize.
- Take a 360-view perspective to create data driven journeys.
- Personas help you to get a hold on the different customer segments in a simplified way.
- Marketing automation can help you to strengthen the relationship with your customer and potential customer by creating relevant and personal communication in an automated way based on the data available.
- Predictive analytics and machine learning can support you to deal with the non-linear journeys, since they cleverly use big data to optimize each individual journey.

PHILIPS

Improving the experience through meaningful innovation

In 1891 Gerard Philips and his father Frederik Philips started a small lightbulb factory in Eindhoven, in the Netherlands. Today, Philips is one of the largest electronics companies in the world employing over 100,000 people in more than 60 countries. Philips is continuously trying to innovate in the areas of electronics, healthcare and lighting, striving to make the world healthier and more sustainable through these innovations. The current tagline 'Innovation and you' reflects Philips' commitment to improving people's lives through meaningful innovation.

Smart toothbrush Sparkly is like a game

Philips fully embraces today's digital world. In particular, the Internet of Things is central to how Philips innovates. It enables Philips to listen to, engage with and take inspiration from customers. Now the Philips products do not only serve customers' needs, but they react to these needs and empower the customer to control their lives better.

The internet of things makes Philips' products more personal, relevant and impactful. But it is not only the product that changes as such, it is the whole customer journey that changes. One of those inspiring innovations in the healthcare division of Philips in this area is the smart toothbrush for kids. True, Philips wasn't the first company to come up with a connected toothbrush, but Philips added another dimension to this. Of course, it is quite a challenge to get children to brush their teeth properly and regularly. At the same time, children love all kinds of game apps. Philips combined these insights into a special Sonicare toothbrush for children aged three and older, that optimized the brushing in a playful way. By changing the brushing habits of the young children, Philips wants to encourage a lifetime of healthy habits.

The Bluetooth-enabled toothbrush comes with a game app starring a little interactive helper named 'Sparkly'. When the child starts brushing, the app reacts by showing Sparkly's mouth as a brushing guide. A virtual toothbrush moves through each quadrant of the mouth, removing remains of food and bacteria and only leaving shining, clean teeth behind. Sparkly makes funny noises and talks to the children to stimulate them to keep on brushing.
Children score points in this game by brushing all four quadrants of their teeth for 30 seconds each, so two minutes in total, which is the standard recommended by most dentists. The points earned can be redeemed so the child can 'play' with their Sparkly; feed them snacks, give them achievement badges, change the colors or dress him up differently. Sparkly has different modes for different age groups, to ensure it stimulates brushing for children of all ages. To make brushing even

more fun, special peel-and-stick stickers are included allowing children to customize the toothbrush. The grip handle is adjusted to make it easy for children to brush without the help of a parent and, last but not least, a program is included to train the child to brush for two minutes: the KidTimer gradually increases the brushing time until the recommended two minutes are reached.

Using data to continuously improve the experience

The app is such a success that children wanted to use the toothbrush over and over again and did not want to finish after the two minutes had passed. For parents this led to a completely new problem, since the children wanted to keep on playing instead of going to bed. Based on both quantitative data and qualitative feedback on this, Philips changed the app and now Sparkly gets tired and collapses after two minutes, encouraging the child to put the brush away and go to bed too.

Philips uses the anonymized data collected to improve the in-app experience, making each brushing journey the most effective journey. To give an example, Sparkly also helps the little brushers to focus on areas forgotten before or harder to reach. And a separate dashboard for the parents allows them to monitor their child's performance and progress. Within this dashboard, the parent can also customize the incentives to keep their children motivated. 98% of parents say it is easier to get children to brush longer and better.

What your company can learn from Philips:

- Use new technologies like IOT to create personal and relevant customer journeys.
- Use gamification techniques to influence customer behavior.
- Connecting devices create additional touchpoints to help your customer reach their goals and thus to help your company improve customer satisfaction.
- Collect more data on how your products are used to improve your product along the way.
- Enable customers to get more quantitative insights in their habits to give them more grip on their lives and make better choices; Philips for example is now giving customers more or less the same insights into their dental health as their dentists.

CATERPILLAR

Personal, relevant interactions based on a 360-degree customer view

The American company Caterpillar, often shortened to Cat, designs and builds heavy machines, engines and financial services, mainly focusing on the construction and mining industry.

Although Caterpillar has its origin in large-scale equipment, it now also sells smaller-scale machines to the construction and agriculture industry. Caterpillar also has a wide product range of clothing and work wear boots.

The company serves its customers via a worldwide network of about 220 independently owned dealers.

Connected machines lead to a massive amount of data

Expanding the product range from large-scale equipment with smaller-scale machines also meant expanding the target audience. The new expansive (potential) customer base led to the strategic decision for Caterpillar to completely focus on the customer and their needs instead of focusing on products. Caterpillar started this transformation journey by looking for new opportunities to create a premium experience which eventually led to growth.

Since the start of the company in 1925, innovation has always been an important theme for Caterpillar. Just as in the past these product innovations were driven by technology, Caterpillar uses technology to understand its customers and optimize its machines and engines from that.

The Internet of Things is key for these innovations. Having the largest population of connected machines and engines in the world enables Caterpillar to collect a massive amount of data. This data directly enables the customer to see in real-time the status of their Caterpillar products and services. Moreover, by adding dealer data as well as public data to the data available at Caterpillar, the organization reached a holistic view of the customer. By using state-of-the-art data analysis, Caterpillar uncovered a lot of information about its customers and created insights in both the sales and the service cycle from its customers' point of view.

Targeted omni-channel communication based on available data

Now that Caterpillar understands its customers better with all this data, relevance of the customer contacts can also be improved. Caterpillar predicts when a customer is likely to buy a new product and then pro-actively reaches out to that customer. Tailor-made messages address the situation of the customer and explain how Caterpillar can help in line with the customer's business objective. In the situation where the customer is currently using a product of one of Caterpillar's competitors, the company emphasizes the

benefits compared to the competitor, both on the quality of the products and on the quality of the services provided.

But not only the content is tailor-made for the customer: so is the channel. All interactions are omni-channel and Caterpillar uses the channel that has proven, in that situation, again using data, to be most effective. Online and social media in particular are increasingly important for the company. Smaller businesses in particular are very active online and Caterpillar continuously pilots new online capabilities in the area of email marketing, social content and ecommerce to target the right customer at the right moment. Though sales consultants remain important in the sales process, these sales conversations are much more effective since Caterpillar has already tracked the online customer journey that took place before the conversation. It knows the sites the customer visited, the content they viewed, the calculations they made, empowering the sales consultant to kick-start the sales conversation. And as you can imagine, the after-sales support works in the same way.

All outcomes of conversations are measured and linked to the customer journey to learn and optimize it continuously. Predictive modeling is key in Caterpillar's customer experience strategy. All available data enables Caterpillar to engage with its customers. And even if this does not lead to a sale straight away, being relevant creates valuable conversations which will lead to sales and renewals in the long term.

Using the complete ecosystem to deliver a consistent experience

Caterpillar created a one-week program to educate its best employees in the area of customer experience. These leaders pass their knowledge on to other parts of the organization.

But Caterpillar does not only focus on its own employees. It understands that the dealers are just as important (and maybe even more important) in order to create an optimal and consistent experience. Clear guiding principles help the dealer to understand how they should engage with the customers. Also, the 360-degree customer view created at Caterpillar is shared with the dealers to make it possible from them to personalize their interactions and content as much as possible too.

All content is made available to the dealers to ensure consistent information worldwide.

Caterpillar assigns multidisciplinary teams, including the dealers, to keep on translating the customer insights into new innovations.

What your organization can learn from Caterpillar:

- Create a 360-degree data view with internal and external data.
- Use customer data in all your interactions to ensure you send the right message via the right channel at the right moments.
- Share your data throughout your organization: ensuring a true omni-channel experience for the customer.
- Don't be afraid to share information within your ecosystem. Two-way sharing of data is beneficial for both parties and leads to much better experiences.

THE NATURAL HISTORY MUSEUM, LONDON

Technology enables

individual journeys

The Natural History Museum is the biggest history museum in the United Kingdom. It cares for more than 80 million specimens spanning billions of years and welcomes more than five million visitors annually. The vision of the museum is broader than simply 'displaying history'; its aim is to "challenge how people think about the natural world – its past, present and future".

Modular tour so customers can construct their own journey

Visiting a museum is something very personal. It's fun, it concerns our 'free time', so we want to have freedom. Feeling 'pushed around' or pressured is not something we want on our day off. The museum seems to understand this, and offers visitors ultimate freedom in choosing their personal journey. They do provide 'modular' tours, so customers can construct their own day tour. Each sub-tour has a name and the average length is specified, so customers can determine how much time they have and what they would like to visit.
For more visual guidance, the different zones in the museum are color-coded and provide the visitor with visual cues. The underwater world can be found in the Blue Zone, the Green Zone displays the planet's evolution and the Red Zone shows how tremendous forces shaped our planet.

The smartphone as ultimate tooling for personalizing customer journeys in the offline world

To get the most out of a museum visit, most of us would agree that a guide is very helpful. He or she sets the scene, explains the main storylines and highlights interesting details. In today's world, we can benefit from having a personal guide in the comfort of our own outfit, as it were: the smartphone. The museum built an app to offer visitors a personal guide experience.

The app uses signal information from the wifi network of the museum, so it can be pinpointed in what area visitors are and what they are looking at. Contextual information about the object they are looking at can be delivered through the app, as well as upselling to specific relevant paid exhibitions. Since more than half of the visitors are international, the multi language option in the app enables these visitors to explore the museum in their native language. This provides an even better customer experience.
The app helps visitors to anticipate possible events, just like a good guide would, such as when you lose those accompanying you, or, the worst case scenario for many parents: your children. It helps you to pick a meeting point when needed. Furthermore, the app suggests you visit the restaurant, but not in a pushy way. It focuses on the well-being of the visitor by stating "if you need to refuel after your prehistoric tour, visit The Kitchen in the Red Zone". This type of messaging feels very warm, and it is close to gamification. It makes you want to go to the restaurant. And of course, always think about the obvious – but very important - basic human needs, such as: "where's the nearest toilet?".
The museum closely monitors how visitors use the app, what their click paths in the app are, the physical paths through the museum are and what decisions they made after viewing specific messages in the app. With this analysis, the customer experience can be improved which will ultimately lead to better business results.

And by having a 'foot in the door' – the app on their phone - the museum has a permanent high-attention interaction channel very close to their customers. This enables the museum to encourage them to keep coming back, or invite friends, share specific events etc.

Using VR in orientation phase to seduce prospects

VR can boost our imagination and help prospects to envision the encounter with the actual product or service. The museum uses VR in a brilliant way: in cooperation with Google, several VR tours are constructed. From the comfort of your own house, you can already have some great experiences 'in' the museum. Sitting on your couch, you can see a seven-meter long skeleton of a Rhomaleosaurus displayed on the wall. As the audio guide explains details about the life of this creature, it starts to come to life and swims off the wall as the museum is suddenly filled with water. You feel like you are the 'prey' the audio guide is talking about! A scary moment that brings so much more experience to the skeletons displayed.

The VR tours are just one piece of content in the impressive online footprint of the museum. Some facts and figures of their huge follower base:

- Twitter: close to 2m followers, almost 20k tweets which are highly liked and retweeted.
- Facebook: >400k likes, 1.2m people have registered their visit and 43k visitors have given a review, of which the average score is an impressive 4.7 out of 5. It displays a lot of their short and 'snackable' YouTube videos about wildlife and 'behind the scenes'.
- Instagram: >100k followers, a lot of beautiful pictures and short videos, very consistent in style.
- Pinterest: >100k followers, various boards, ranging from specific collections to behind the scenes and posters of the museum.

Why are these numbers so interesting? It shows that a lot of people care for the content that the museum is spreading. The content is medium-appropriate, most of it is short and simple, and it leaves you begging for more. When a person follows the museum online, it can frequently see pieces from the museum and this can lead to a closer relationship with it, thus potentially leading to more visits. Also, as the high number of reviews shows, people are very enthusiastic about the museum and they share their experiences on Facebook, which is then visible to their friends as well. This can be seen as a strong example of customer loyalty.

What your organization can learn from the Natural History Museum:

- Think about how technology can support your customers in creating personal journeys.
- Use the power of a mobile device to become as close to your customer as possible.
- Create several calls to action in multiple places during the journey to contribute to your business objectives.
- Enrich the customer journey by linking the online and offline experience.
- Think about where the customer journey truly starts. The Natural History Museum cleverly uses VR to start the journey at home.
- Interact with customers whenever relevant in the customer journey, also on external channels like Facebook.

NETFLIX

Data usage to predict the success

Netflix is the world's leading internet television network. Its streaming service allows members to instantly watch television shows and movies on their personal devices. Starting as a small online movie rental company, Netflix is currently used in 190 countries by 93.8 million members. Netflix's success is primarily based on one aspect: the usage of data.

Netflix uses data to predict what customers will enjoy watching

Netflix does not just pick the licenses for movies and television shows at random. Licensing movies and shows are expensive, so Netflix has to find out which items its members will enjoy the most. Over 800 developers are continuously finding ways to maximize the impact of data in every aspect of their business. They collect and monitor data of all users in an attempt to understand viewing habits. Based on a thorough understanding and combination of data, Netflix tries to predict what customers will enjoy watching. In this way, analytics enable Netflix to make better, more informed decisions and improve their services. Data is used for three different purposes:

1 Product selections.
2 Personalized offering.
3 New content.

Netflix gathers data on a larger scale to identify user trends and create a good understanding of the overall engagement of a show or movie. Important criteria for this are the number of views, the completion rate (e.g. how many people finished the first season?), common cut points (when did people drop out?) and the time gap between different episodes. Based on the overall engagement, Netflix decides to cancel or (re)start a new show or movie. For example, if the data shows 70% of the users watched all seasons available of a cancelled show, Netflix might consider restarting the show due to the likelihood that customers will watch the new season.

More than 125 million TV hours a day are used to enrich customer profiles

Netflix' main goal is to increase the frequency and intensity of streaming, to prevent customers from cancelling their membership. To increase the usage of its service, Netflix tries to help members to discover new movies and TV shows they will enjoy. For this purpose, Netflix fills its analytics with sophisticated customer behavior.

As part of the on-boarding process, Netflix asks new users to rate their interest in movie genres and rate any movie they have already seen to get a first understanding of customer preferences. To enrich customer profiles, Netflix looks at more than 125 million hours of TV shows and movies per day. Personal data not only comprises the number and type of views per day, Netflix also monitors the specific day and time of the day shows are watched, and on what devices. Moreover, Netflix captures data concerning when you pause, rewind and fast forward, your ratings, searches, and your browsing and scrolling behavior. Even your preferences on titles, colors and covers are monitored. All this data will be transformed into personalization algorithms that aim to accurately predict what users will watch next. And with success, 75% of viewer activity is based on these personal suggestions.

Decisions on new content based on customer insights

Next to its role as distributor of streaming content, Netflix utilizes its rich database to add new content. Commissioning two seasons of House of Cards, comprising of 26 episodes, for $100 million without a pilot may seem like a risky investment. However, based on its data, Netflix already knew the new series would become a big success. House of Cards had three key ingredients: David Fincher (director and producer), Kevin Spacey (leading role) and the British version of House of Cards. All of them were popular on Netflix and had a high completion rate.

By combining these factors, Netflix found out there existed a large potential target group for House of Cards without rolling a pilot.

As well as the decision on the investment, Netflix also used data in the promotion of the series. They made ten different trailers for each type of Netflix member. Each member received a personalized trailer tailored to their specific interests. For example, people interested in Kevin Spacey films saw a trailer featuring him, while others saw a trailer featuring David Fincher.

The data based approach turned House of Cards into a great success and it is ranked among the most influential series in television history, boosting the number of new subscribers at Netflix.

What your organization can learn from Netflix:

- Build a data driven organization in which all decisions are based on data.
- Use insights and data to revise your product portfolio in line with your customers' needs and create customer profiles as a foundation for more personalized communication.
- Data sources, opportunities and customer needs are continuously evolving. Start with the data points available and create a flexible analytics infrastructure to refine your analytics in line with changes in the analytics climate.

CHINA RAPID FINANCE

Multi-channel, multi-data

Shanghai-based China Rapid Finance (CRF) began operations in 2001 as a provider of technology to analyze Chinese consumer credit for large financial institutions. Ever since, approximately 100 million credit cards have been issued to Chinese consumers by using China Rapid Finance's technology. In 2010, CRF decided to use their expertise on sophisticated data usage and their knowledge of the Chinese credit market to start their own marketplace lending platform.

A clever use of big data to create new business models

Ever since the start of the company in 2001, CRF has been specialized in credit analytics. First as a service for China's leading banks, and, since 2010, CFR has improved the technology and uses it in their own platform to serve customers directly. CRF is now one of the largest peer-to-peer lending platforms, which lend money to customers without the interference of a bank.

Of the total Chinese population of 1.4 billion people, 800 million are financially active of which 300 million have credit records at the central bank of China. That means there are about 500 million Chinese people that can't borrow money from traditional financial organizations, although many of them have stable incomes. CFR defines this group as China's Emerging Middle-Class Mobile Active Consumers: EMMA. EMMA is typically under 30 years old, urban, well-educated and mobile active. In the past, these creditworthy borrowers didn't have access to consumer credit since they weren't logged in the database of the Central Credit Bureau. However, unlike their saver parents, these millennials are much more likely to apply for a loan.

CRF offers a mobile platform that automatically scores the consumer creditworthiness based on data from financial institutions, social networks and anti-fraud information collected from Chinese cities. Each individual gets its own risk profile based on this data. The data from the financial institutions is provided by institutional and payment system partners of CRF as well as by CRF's own credit data developed over the years. Clever partnerships with online travel agencies, online group-buy and shopping platforms, online gaming companies, online e-commerce platforms and payment service providers enable CRF to get into contact with EMMA consumers.

Create long-lasting relationships by targeting the right customers

CRF does not want to be in contact with all visitors of these sites, only with the creditworthy ones. Since CRF gets a massive amount of unstructured data - amongst others online social network data, search data and e-commerce purchase data - from the online partnerships, they can select the best consumers. Exclusive algorithms analyze the data to pre-screen all possible borrowers and select the ones with the lowest risks.

So, these online partners enable CRF to get into contact with these pre-qualified EMMA consumers. To illustrate: based on the available data, CRF was able to isolate 50 million users of one of the social media platforms of Tencent, the giant Chinese internet company, who had a high creditworthiness based on the predictive analyses of CRF. These users were offered a small loan of about the average salary of one week and they could easily accept these offers with just a few clicks.

CRF is continuously optimizing their algorithms to make them better. However, to be eligible for the automated credit decision-making, CRF only offers smaller loans. Only when a customer has built a decent credit history with multiple smaller CRF loans do they get access to larger loans such as auto and home loans or credit cards. These loans require additional data verification and CRF maintains special data verification centers across China to approve these loans. Again, based on algorithms, not on the decision of the employee. At these data verification centers, EMMAs can quickly apply for larger and longer-term loans. This combination of online and offline loan approval enables CRF to build a longer-term relationship with their target audience while minimizing risk.

What your organization can learn from China Rapid Finance:

- Partner with companies who have large customer bases to get access to relevant customer data to create sophisticated predictive models that select the right customers to target and to get access to these customers too.
- Make it as easy as possible for your customers to purchase your products.
- Create more simple versions of products to be offered via online channels.
- Combine online and offline channels to nurture the relationship with your customers.

T-MOBILE

A new platform to anchor itself in the lives of customers

T-Mobile, part of Deutsche Telekom, is an international telecoms operator. Worldwide, T-Mobile has close to 230 million subscribers, making T-Mobile the fourth-largest multinational telecom operator.

In the fast changing environment of telecom operators, the company has reinvented their added value towards both its B2B and B2C customers. The need for a solid strategy is high, because the position of T-Mobile as mobile-only player is less solid in the market than the position of all-in-one parties that can rely on their quad play (i.e. internet, TV, fixed line telephone at home and mobile telephone services) which results in a higher exit barrier for customers.

T-Mobile wants to improve people's lives

T-Mobile want to build on and focus on what they do best: they are an expert in everything mobile. By using this expertise, T-Mobile wants to improve people's lives. They focus on all new technological innovations, many taking place on mobile, and conclude: all these innovations improve human lives by making life more fun, saver, easier or healthier. T-Mobile feels responsible for speeding up this progress. Their claim: the future is made together, so we dare you to live forward with us.

In order to facilitate this acceleration, T-Mobile created the platform Live Forward: a collection of trends and technology news items that inspire and inform about the world of tomorrow.

The platform can be seen as a local coffee house, where people come to chat with each other, but where people are also inspired by news articles.

T-Mobile invites both customers and non-customers to think about next steps in technology, and to send in any questions they have regarding technology. They also invite entrepreneurs to explain their needs. This open attitude creates a sense of belonging, and it results in longer and stronger customer relationships.

Stop campaign-based thinking

Live Forward is more than just a platform: it is the central point in the entire strategy.

A big impact of the new strategy can be found in the marketing department: marketing has changed from campaign-based thinking to 'always on' mindset. There is no more time for making long-term content calendars since technology news changes very rapidly. Besides that, consumers prefer relationships over 'campaigns'.

Besides the 'always on' mindset, marketers have learned to work with profiles instead of customer segments. The data of online behavior enables T-Mobile to gain a more accurate profile of their customers, and it makes more sense to use these profiles instead of customer segment and personas' 'gut feeling'.

Live Forward changes T-Mobile: more agile and 'always on'

Quick tests and rapid improvement of new services and propositions is part of this new way of working. T-Mobile wants to launch products and propositions faster since this is required by the market. One example of the more agile method of proposition development, are the 'time limited data bundles': an innovation on 'usage limited bundles'. On weekend festivals, users had the possibility to purchase a large data bundle just for the weekend, in order to share all photos via social media with their friends.

Another example is the design sprint T-Mobile conducted on using a chatbot in Messenger. A multidisciplinary team created a working prototype in only five days.

Testing propositions like this takes place with 'real people', instead of wasting time on lengthy testing procedures.

Live Forward supports existing innovative projects by empowering customers and employees

T-Mobile wants to help its customers by providing expertise and craftsmanship, instead of just financing projects or innovations. They do so by supporting existing projects as well as starting new projects. They have already completed many great projects to help society with technology, and now it has a central stage where these activities can be displayed. For example, people can participate in classes about how to use technology such as smartphones.

One of the projects that is currently supported is the use of the mobile sensors in phones to detect when an elderly person has fallen and needs help. The phone can detect whether it is only the phone that fell, or when the owner of the phone has also fallen and needs help.

All employees from the entire organization are involved: everybody can write on the platform about projects or activities they do in the spirit of Live Forward. They are owners of the content and are also entitled to responding to reactions themselves.

Biggest win so far: consumers become ambassadors

What are the results? First of all the negative sentiment of T-Mobile is dropping really fast. Only 0.8% of the customer comments are negative. Consumers even start to defend T-Mobile in online discussions where other consumers talk negatively about the brand or services provided.

With the new strategy, T-Mobile wants to improve their presence in the lives of customers (B2C and B2B2C) and prospects. This seems a solid strategy to stay relevant in this fast changing environment. By helping people with technological innovations, T-Mobile creates a positive vibe and this will result in higher brand loyalty. The future will show how this affects their market share, but the first results look promising.

What your organization can learn from T-Mobile:

- Think about the changing consumer needs in a broader context and find ways to be relevant. This should still be in line with your brand values, but might be much broader than the product you offer.
- Dare to bring innovations to market without elaborate testing upfront. Create prototypes to gain true insights and speed up the time-to-market.
- Think in relationships instead of in campaigns.
- Educate customers in the new desired behavior and from there, let them actively participate in the development of the strategy.

Chapter 4

KEEP ON INNOVATING

HOW EMBRACING NEW TECHNOLOGIES AND PHILOSOPHIES CAN SPEED UP REALIZING BETTER EXPERIENCES

In the previous chapter we discussed how data and new techniques help you to manage customer journeys, behind the customer's back, as it were. In this chapter, we will discuss how techniques change the actual customer experience, visible to the customer. This chapter deals with the most influential technologies regarding customer experience and sets apart how organizations are getting closer to the customer, how machines are replacing human contact in the journey and how the journey becomes a natural conversation.

Next to new technologies, new philosophies are quickly being accepted and implemented by companies to deal with the new technologies and keep optimizing the customer experiences rapidly. We address what we believe are the two most important philosophies: the agile way of working and design thinking.

Closer to the customer through new contacts

New technologies enable you to come closer to the customer. This trend already started with telephony, enabling customers to have conversations with organizations without having to visit a store, branch or office. Computers and the internet made it possible for organizations to come even closer to the customer and led to the 24/7 economy.

But as technology evolves and the customer journey is fully digitized, this exponentially increases the number of interactions between an organization and its customers. Developments in the digital and mobile channels have in particular caused an increase in the number of interactions between a customer and organizations. These interactions offer numerous opportunities to make the relationship more personal again. Think of banking apps, which enable banks to have small interactions with their customers daily.

This digitization is not hype. It is a long-lasting movement for which the future impact will go much further that we can imagine right now. New technologies enable organizations to come closer and closer. We have evolved from a desktop computer to the laptop to the tablet to smartphones to the smart watch. The smart watch is one of the most common forms of wearable: a smart electronic device that can be worn on the body as an implant or accessory. Other well-known examples of wearables are the Fitbit system, also worn on the wrist, or Google Glass.

Wearables are, as the name suggests, worn by the user. Nowadays, however, we also see examples of technology planted inside a human (biohackables, to improve our human body) or technology you can swallow ('swallowables', like a smart pill).

Wearables create a constant interaction between the wearable and the user, since there is no need to turn the device on or off. There is a constant flow of data and all these devices collecting and exchanging data together is what we call the Internet of Things (IoT): the network of connected or smart devices that can be sensed and/or controlled remotely across the network infrastructure. This leads to a direct integration of the physical world and computers. By making these wearables part of your customer experience, you create a way of being always close to the customer, both physically and due to the fact that you create a better 360 degree view of the customer. All these connected devices lead to a mass of customer data which organizations can use to optimize and individualize their experiences (as discussed in Chapter 3).

Machines replacing humans for direct contact

Digitization is a broad term, quite often used in the context of automatization. Organizations focus on replacing manual processes by automated ones, for example marketing automation, as discussed in chapter 3. Automation is mostly done to reduce costs and improve efficiency, however, as you can imagine, an automated and thus faster and error-free process is also beneficial to the customer.

Robots are maybe the clearest example of machines entirely replacing humans. Although in a manufacturing context we have seen all kinds of robots for some time now, today robots are becoming more common in a customer-facing context as well. Chatbots make you believe you are chatting with a customer service agent, while it is a machine you are talking to. Self-service check-ins at the airport are another example of how technology is replacing service agents. But we haven't seen the most far-reaching form of robot yet. In the future, more and more human interactions will be replaced by an interaction between a human and a machine. Think about drones delivering your mail package instead of the mailman. Or self-driving cars making taxi drivers obsolete.

What is the effect on customer experience? In general, customers will get a more consistent experience since the organization is in full control of the process and the means to deliver the experience. Most likely the experience will also be improved because of the higher speed at which it will be delivered. And since machines don't have to deal with working hours, processes become available 24/7 whenever it suits the customer. Since customers will only accept being serviced by a 'machine' if this leads to at least the same experience, organizations have to redesign the customer journey in the most optimal way for the customer. And lastly, as discussed in Chapter 3, when machine learning is added to the bots, the experience will become more personal and relevant: yet another reason to believe the robotics trend will lead to improved experiences.

Conversational experiences

As interactions become smarter, we see another interesting thing happening. The customer journey is not in websites or apps, but tapping and swiping is being replaced by a familiar interface from the past: conversations.

Take KLM as an example. They were the first airline worldwide to enable their customers to receive all their flight information via Facebook Messenger. Customers receive their itinerary via the chat, which notifies them when they can check in. The biggest advantage of using Facebook Messenger however, is that next to reviewing all this information, customers can directly contact a KLM service agent in the same environment whenever they have a question. Providing permanent context leads to a natural, pleasant and frictionless conversation, instead of receiving your boarding pass via e-mail and then being linked to the frequently asked questions part on the website or a call center for more information.

And since customers are getting used to being engaged in multiple conversations simultaneously, using Facebook Messenger has another advantage. KLM lets the customer decide on the speed at which they want to react. Conversational apps like Facebook Messenger are rapidly evolving to generate what we call 'conversational experiences': they let customers experience the whole customer journey as a natural dialog. From buying products to sending payments, from asking questions to changing details.

And this is not only limited to text-based messaging. Apple introduced voice-based messaging technology Siri to make the use of your iPhone a conversational experience: instead of swiping and tapping, you simply tell Siri what you want to do. As Siri also shows, the agent on the other side of the conversation does not need to be a human person. Artificial intelligence makes it possible to use bots for the dialogs. In fact, conversational experiences will only be most optimal when these 'virtual agents' are used. As discussed before, there is so much big data available nowadays that only technologies such as machine learning will enable organizations to truly think contextually. Take the KLM Facebook Messenger service as an example. Of course, a human service agent can provide perfect information about how to get to the airport, but only a virtual agent can tell you exactly when to leave based on current traffic jams, strikes, the average speed of your car and the fact that you also have to stop at the gas station since your tank is almost empty.

The agile way of working needed to respond to all these changes

While existing organizations are digitizing their customer experience step by step, new unexpected and disrupting competitors are entering the market, using new technologies as the backbone of their organization and, in this way, surprising customers with completely different and better customer journeys. How should existing organizations react? How can new technologies improve their business just as quickly as they do for newcomers? An agile way of working is commonly used for these existing organizations to be able to respond quickly to new technologies.

'Agile' is a philosophy describing principles of a new, iterative way of working in which you deliver a valuable result for the customer after each iteration. This result could be, for example, a product, a service, a campaign, a webpage or a new release of an app. It will not be the ideal end state, but it is the so-called minimum viable product (MVP): the most basic version of the product (or service, campaign, etc.) to be of value to the customer.

Let's take the manufacturing of a car as an example to illustrate this. Only a set of wheels is of no value to the customer if he or she wants to get from A to Z. Some organizations would argue that if you create a step out of these wheels, or a bike, this customer could get from A to Z, so a step could be the MVP. However, we believe if you truly look at the customer's needs it is not only going from A to Z, but at a certain speed and with a certain comfort (e.g. sitting dry, being able to bring another person). So the MVP would be a kind of car only focusing on sitting comfortably to get from A to Z quickly. After releasing the MVP, the car would become more and more comfortable in the next iterations. Again, each iteration is of true added value for the customer.

Because of all these iterations, the agile way of working offers a lot of flexibility to react to the changing environment and advancing insights.
The agile philosophy originates from an IT-related project. However, nowadays it is commonly used throughout the whole organization. Though the original agile manifesto focused more on the IT side, there is also an agile marketing manifesto to support, amongst others, your customer experience activities:

1. Validated learning over opinions and conventions.

2. Customer focused collaboration over silos and hierarchy.

3. Adaptive and iterative campaigns over 'big bang' campaigns.

4. The process of customer discovery over static prediction.

5. Flexible vs. rigid planning.

6. Responding to change over following a plan.

7. Many small experiments over a few large bets.

Figure 4.1: How to build a minimum viable product

1   2   3   4

1   2   3   4

1   2   3   4

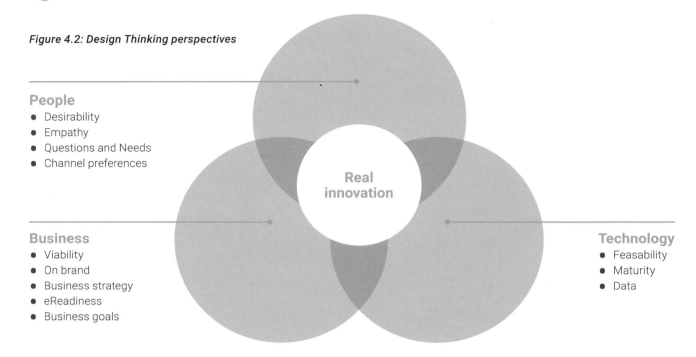

Figure 4.2: Design Thinking perspectives

People
- Desirability
- Empathy
- Questions and Needs
- Channel preferences

Business
- Viability
- On brand
- Business strategy
- eReadiness
- Business goals

Real innovation

Technology
- Feasability
- Maturity
- Data

Human-centered customer journeys request Design Thinking

With the agile philosophy, Design Thinking is another way of thinking used by organizations to deal with the rapidly changing world around them.

Design thinking has been made famous by the company IDEO, which uses the following definition: "Design thinking is a human-centered approach to innovation that draws from the designer's toolkit to integrate the needs of people, the possibilities of technology, and the requirements for business success." Design thinking is a way of thinking which aims for a deep understanding of human behavior and customer needs in order to develop actual problem hypotheses and generate as many solutions as possible.

A challenge is a 'how to' question in which we focus on a certain type of customer in a certain situation; for example, how to make the installation of a device for new customers as easy as possible.

Redesigning the customer journey can mean redesigning a single contact moment, but generally, the problem to be solved is linked to a small set of contact moments: a 'mini' customer journey. In our example, optimizing the installation of a new device might not only mean improving the installation itself, but also setting expectations upfront when the customer buys the device, or sending an automatic message afterwards once the device has been successfully installed.

In the process of design thinking you always follow three steps to get the best solutions for your challenge:
- inspiration
- ideation
- implementation.

Figure 4.3: Three steps design thinking

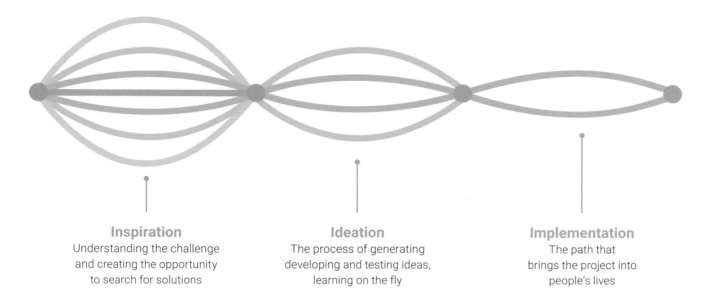

Inspiration
Understanding the challenge
and creating the opportunity
to search for solutions

Ideation
The process of generating
developing and testing ideas,
learning on the fly

Implementation
The path that
brings the project into
people's lives

 1   *Inspiration to understand the challenge and get inspired*

The inspiration phase is all about opening up to new insights regarding the challenge. We expand our viewpoint by gathering information from as many sources of inspiration as possible; from people, business and technology point of view, for instance via customer interviews, customer safaris (where teams go out to experience the realities of customer interaction and experience) questionnaires, data analyses or technology scans. Design thinking helps you to focus on the customer and their situation to reach a broader perspective on the challenge we are facing.

To ensure we are able to define concrete solutions however, we need our challenge to be focused. We select a certain target group (a persona), use customer insights or the design principles (see Chapter 1) to narrow the scope of solutions.

2   *Ideation to generate, develop, iterate and test ideas*

In the ideation phase, we want to create validated prototypes, ready for implementation. In order to do so, we complete a couple of design sprints.

A design sprint is a relatively short but intense period of time where an idea is developed into a validated prototype by a design team of diverse stakeholders.

Starting from a persona or proto persona, a design challenge and design principles, together we visualize and develop ideas to innovate on specific touchpoints in a mini-journey.

In a series of weeks, we validate visualized ideas with real customers through lean testing methodologies and based on test results, we iterate and improve ideas, learn from failure and refine our prototype to make it ready for implementation.

The Ideation phase is usually kicked-off by a so-called design studio. During a one-day workshop, a multidisciplinary design team defines as many possible solutions to our challenge as possible.

At the end of the day we select the best ideas based on expected impact for the customer, competitive advantage, link with brand values, contribution to business objectives, investments and feasibility that we want to explore in more depth.

The design studio has four crucial ingredients:
- Proto persona/ persona: the person we are designing for
- Design Challenge: short description of the problem we are trying to solve
- Design Principles: limits of the challenge (see Chapter 1).
- Design team: 5-7 stakeholders from different backgrounds, including the customer

The design studio is the official starting point for the Design Sprint. During the first sprint, we concretize the selected ideas and visualize them in such a way that customers will get a clear understanding of our idea. We perform user tests to test the ideas with customers. We test the perception, feeling and emotion, relevance and functionality of the prototypes.

By using prototypes, we don't have to rely on the imagination of customers, but we can see their behavior and reactions. Therefore, prototypes improve the quality of the feedback on the idea.

During the second design sprint, we adjust our idea based on customer feedback. Again, we visualize, test and collect feedback.

This iterative process can be repeated as frequently as needed, but mostly 2 or 3 sprints should do in order to generate a prototype ready for implementation.

3   *Implementation to bring the ideas to life*

Once we have learned enough, we want to implement our ideas. Nowadays, most organizations have implemented agile ways of working to ensure short iteration implementation, continuously adding value to the customer. So, design thinking and an agile way of working are often used together.

Key take-aways:

- New technologies enable you to get closer to your customers and get more valuable contacts.
- Machines substitute human contacts nowadays, and since these technologies are becoming ever smarter they can provide a better experience than humans can.
- Customer journeys are turning into natural conversations between customers and organizations.
- In order to respond quickly to changing technological opportunities, organizations should embrace the agile philosophy and work in short iterations.
- To address specific customer needs, human-centered design thinking can help you. By defining actual customer challenges on a touchpoint or a mini-journey, you can generate as many ideas as possible.

TD BANK

Bank Human

TD Bank is one of the ten largest banks in the United States offering banking, insurance, brokerage and investment banking services throughout the eastern part of the US. TD stands for Toronto-Dominion, the Canadian multinational Toronto-Dominion Bank, the parent company of TD Bank. TD Bank calls itself 'America's Most Convenient Bank'. It serves more than 8.5 million customers through its network of close to 1,300 stores (TD Bank is recognized for its retail approach to banking, so does not use the term 'branches').

TD CENTRE

TD Canada Trust

Destination, design and data are the key pillars in the TD Bank's strategy

TD Bank claims to 'bank human'. If something matters to humans, it matters to TD Bank. TD Bank strives for a unified TD customer experience, to prove its humanity to its customers. In order to do so, TD Bank set a clear strategy with three main pillars: destination, design and data.
Destination is about the end goal the customer wants to achieve. The customer experience should be designed in such a way that the customer can easily move from one channel to another depending on their choice and the context they are in. An omni-channel experience is an important prerequisite for this.

Design is the second pillar. TD Bank starts all internal processes by taking the customer as the starting point. They think about how the customer wants to interact with TD Bank's products and services to reach their destination and act accordingly. Data is about analytics and collecting insights on the customer's behavior. Both the intended and the actual behavior are measured across all products and all channels so TD Bank can design the optimal customer experience.

TD Bank is human in everything it does

TD Bank proves they bank human in several areas:
- Over 1,300 locations for your convenience and they have the longest opening hours, so if you are a little early or a little late, you are still on time. The doors also remain open during the weekend, since that is the moment you have time to get things done. However, during some holidays the stores are closed 'so the dedicated TD Bank team can spend time with their friends and families'.
- They surprise you with conveniences like letting you bring your dog or keep the pen you use to write with when you're done. Or getting a TD branded lollipop. These little things truly make a difference and TD designs the experience around little things like this.
- The people working for TD Bank are extremely customer oriented and will go the extra mile for you.

- Mobile banking brings you the convenience of taking care of your own business whenever and wherever you want. So, whatever your destination as TD calls it, you will get there.
- Unconventional emotional campaigns, for example turning ATM into Automated Thank you Machines, where selected customers were given gifts as part of TD Bank's annual customer appreciation day. The emotional and heart-warming movies showing the reactions of the customers went viral and added a lot to the positive image of TD Bank.

Digitization in a human way

Though TD Bank optimizes the customer experience throughout all channels, of course digital is key for the customer and thus for the bank. Customers expect to be able to do a large part of the customer journey by themselves. Yet they don't always feel comfortable to do so. TD Bank therefore believes they need to improve the relationship they have with the customer by providing education and personal guidance.

After digital, the human component of stores and phone needs to be adjusted to the digital journey to offer support and value-adding services whenever needed. TD Bank spends a lot of time talking to their customers on a regular basis to understand what their needs are. They found out that the underlying themes don't change over time. Being the most convenient bank as they strive to be is still relevant to their customers. However, what does this mean in the digital era? As a result, TD Bank spends ample time looking at the customer journey and finding ways to improve it.

Own and external data gives TD Bank deep insight into its customers

As mentioned, data is an important element for helping TD Bank to get customer insights. The bank gathers operational data: customer interactions, transactions, feedback. It then adds external online data to this to create an even more complete customer journey, especially non-banking data, such as data showing how consumers are buying on Amazon.com, or what they are talking about on social media, which gives TD bank deep insights into the 'pain points' of customers.

TD Bank also uses design thinking to improve these pain points. A multidisciplinary team thinks about a problem the customer is facing and forces them to come up with ideas that really wow the customer. New ways to improve the customer experience, taking the customer as the main starting point and thereby ensuring that all improvements are in line with the ambition of TD Bank: to remain the most convenient bank.

What your organization can learn from TD Bank:

- Set a clear ambition that everybody in the organization understands and ensure everything is in line with that.
- Translate your brand value into as many aspects of the customer journey as possible.
- Challenge yourself to be distinctive even if your industry seems to leave little room to be distinctive.
- Enrich your own data with external data to get even better insights.
- Use design thinking to come up with out-of-the-box solutions.

AMAZON

Creating valuable experiences through customer obsession

Amazon's vision is to be 'Earth's most customer-centric company'. In their own words, they wish "to build a place where people can come to find and discover anything they might want to buy online." Originally founded as an online bookstore, today Amazon operates websites in different countries. And not just to sell books. They have since expanded their offering to dozens of product lines, ranging from diverse categories such as beauty, automotive, media, toys, sports, garden utilities, and "just about anything else" – including Amazon's own media carriers, such as the Kindle e-reader, Amazon Echo, and Fire TV.

Amazon is creating true individual moments by using technology and data

Amazon is renowned for its consistent customer obsession, through which it manages to excel not only at standard moments and moments of truth, but also by reinforcing its central brand value at every important customer touch point. By means of this strong customer focus – treating customers as their guests and making excellent use of technology and data for the benefit of their customers – Amazon is able to create true individual moments. Another element to Amazon's success in delivering an excellent experience to their 225 million customers is a strong and consistent focus on customer satisfaction, starting with a customer-first company culture and perfected throughout the entire journey right up to the last customer touch point. As a result, Amazon consistently ranks high in pretty much any international customer experience index, including Foresee, Temkin, and Forrester's. Customer-centricity is promoted throughout the company among all employees and in every department. This includes CEO Jeff Bezos, who has to work customer service lines for two days every two years to help permeate the organization with the importance of putting the customer first. Amazon's strong focus on the customer is reinforced by its mission statement as mentioned above, driving day-to-day decisions at every level of the company, right down to Amazon's logo which includes a customer smile.

Convenience: making technology and data work to serve the customer's needs

Since the heart of its service is web-based, Amazon focuses on creating an effortless online customer experience. For example, 1-Click ordering is automatically enabled after customers place their first order with Amazon. Selecting the 'Buy now with 1-Click' option on any product page will automatically charge an order to the payment method in place and ship it to the address associated with the customer's 1-Click settings. This ensures that the checkout process is fast and simple and prevents customers from having to re-enter payment or shipping information.

Whenever a customer needs support or wishes to return an item, Amazon's customer service is always readily available. Amazon offers many self-service tools and additional live support channels such as web chat and email.

Serving 225 million customers, Amazon is able to capture a huge amount of data and use it to continuously improve its service to its customers. Even though the goal might ultimately be commercial, the use of data always starts and ends with the potential benefits for customers. Even when the customer isn't aware of it, for instance with pricing automation, through which Amazon ensures the customer always gets the best possible deal.

Probably the most common example of how data use may benefit customers is Amazon's use of real-time browsing and buying history in order to recommend products to users. The 'Frequently Bought Together' and 'Customers Who Bought This Item Also Bought' sections, displaying what other customers purchased, make for a highly personalized experience. This way Amazon helps customers by limiting the endless number of choices available, which strengthens its relationship with its customers and inspires them to come back again and shop for more.

Drones to deliver packages

Amazon is always pushing to move forward. In 2014, Amazon acquired a patent for anticipatory shipping, which makes it possible to ship products to storage facilities in areas where sales are anticipated to be high, shortening shipping time for the customer. The patent also makes it possible to ship products to the customer's address, even before he or she has actually ordered and paid for a product, on the basis of customer data such as search data, previous buys, wish lists, and the time a user hovers their mouse over a specific product. At the same time, Amazon is working on Prime Air, a future parcel delivery service that uses drones to deliver packages to customers in 30 minutes or less. Through this and other innovations, Amazon keeps looking for new opportunities to improve the lives of their customers in any way they can think of, even if it takes some time to get the required regulatory support.

What other organization can learn from Amazon:

- Be truly customer-obsessed and ensure you base your decisions on your customers' experiences.
- Make sure that all employees (including the CEO!) engage in real contact with customers every now and then, e.g. by working the customer service lines.
- Focus on long-term relationships with customers.
- Make the experience fast and easy.
- Use data to personalize the experience to benefit your customer.
- Keep on innovating by using new technologies.

WECHAT

Using mobile to improve and orchestrate the customer journey

WeChat was founded in 2011 in China, and usage has exploded to 762 million monthly active users. This app started out as 'yet another chat app', but it has quickly evolved to the 'one app to rule them all' since it provides users with endless possibilities to interact with millions of organizations (both service and sales). One could even say, it is becoming 'the one app that facilitates (mobile) customer journeys' in China. The penetration in China is close to 100%. Outside of China, the app grows rapidly as well, as there are currently 70 million users outside of China. More than 50% of the users open the app more than 10 times a day.

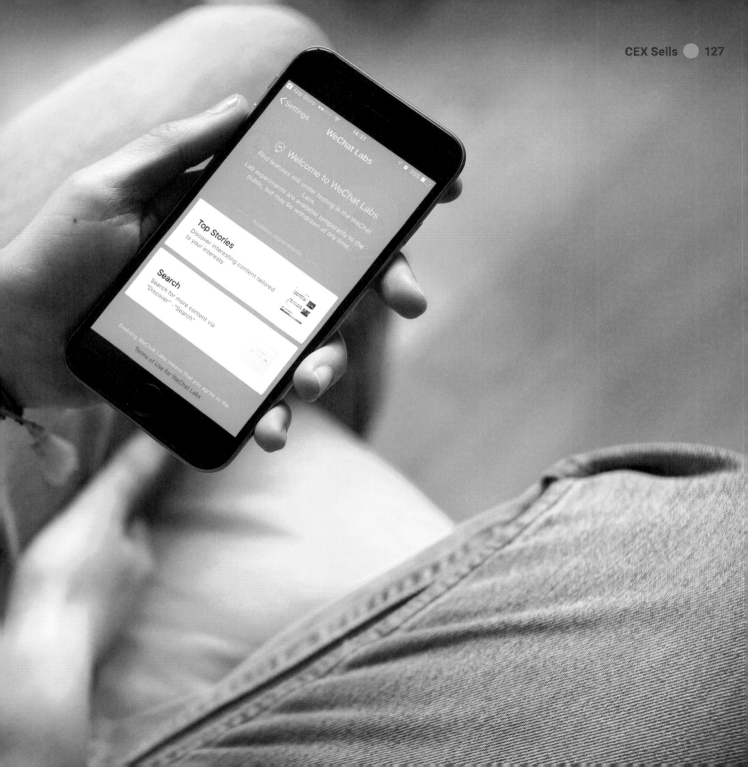

Functionalities for every moment and action in a customer's life

WeChat realizes that mobile is the enabler to stay connected and serve your customers. We cannot live without our phones anymore: we start our day with them, during our day we might check our phones around 200 times, and very often, it is the last thing we hold on to when we go to sleep. Combined with the fact that smartphones are becoming very smart, fully sensored mini-computers, the opportunity is quite obvious. And yet, many organizations do not yet reap the possibilities that are created. WeChat wants to help users with every action or need in their lives. So how does WeChat attract and entertain all these active users?

The main ingredient is the possibility for other organizations to interact and serve their customers through the WeChat app. WeChat started out with their chat functionality, and added other core-customer-interaction-functionalities along the way. These functionalities are open for other organizations (through APIs such as payments, location, direct messages, voice messages, users IDs), and this way, WeChat becomes a platform on which consumers can interact (communicate, service and sales) with millions of companies. WeChat functions almost like a mobile operating system on its own.

Some examples of functionalities: WeChat offers chat, both in text as in speech, with other humans and with bots. WeChat provides mobile payments (the so-called 'Wallet'): users can pay for services or goods, transfer money, make donations. Another example is that you can play games, recognize music and access fitness tracker data. The bottom line is that you do not need to leave the app for anything! Your entire day can take place without leaving the app once.

Convenience drives experience which drives usage

Since organizations can use all functionalities that WeChat provides, different types of customer experience apps exist within the app. For example remote control: LINQ hotel enables their guests to decide on lighting and climate control of their room via WeChat by scanning a QR-code. M4JAM is a micro-jobbing service in South-Africa which offers small jobs to WeChatters, such as taking surveys or doing mystery shopping. And there is a second screen experience: Big Brother Mzansi offers viewers of Big Brother in South Africa a way to view extra material and vote for their favorites, chat with other fans and interact with the contestants.

The functionalities keep evolving, and for many organizations, WeChat becomes the primary interaction-app/platform, despite their own apps. Already, WeChat holds over ten million third-party apps. Some start-ups go live first on WeChat before they launch their separate app. It enables a quick test with many users and the experiences for users are more personalized due to the stored historical data. As a result, they very often lead to more sales.

Mobile commerce integration as a growth hacker for WeChat

A very interesting growth hack for WeChat comes from the payment functionalities that WeChat offers to organizations and its customers. The payments take place within the WeChat Wallet: a menu for users with several payment connections and providers that users can use after they enter their payment credentials. One in five users already has their Wallet activated, so they can use it within the app for all kinds of purchases. All accounts within WeChat can benefit from this frictionless way of paying, and this boosts growth even more. It is the perfect example of smooth customer experience: enabling your customers to easily buy the products and services they need. Win-win: your customer is happy, and you achieve more sales. What more can you wish for!

What your organization can learn from WeChat:

- Mobile technology can be a connector between the online and offline world. In China, traditions are very important. One of them is the giving of money in a red envelope, for special occasions such as New Year, weddings or the birth of a baby. WeChat has created a functionality that enables users to send each other money in a digital red envelope.
- Keep communication with your customers simple and accessible. The WeChat communication and openness is very down to earth and friendly.
- Experimenting with user functions in order to keep customers engaged. The 'shake' functionality enables consumers to connect with new people they have never met. With the 'message in a bottle' functionality, users can pick up or throw out a 'message in a bottle'. The message goes to totally random WeChat users around the world.

CARREFOUR

Spicing up the in-store retail experience with humanoid robot 'Pepper'

Retailer Carrefour, established in 1959 in Annecy, France, is considered one of the most recognizable retail brands in the world. With more than 12,000 stores and e-commerce sites, a presence in more than 30 countries, and more than 13 million customers around the world every day, Carrefour is a company that has every reason to be at the forefront of customer experience innovation.

Technology is at the heart of Carrefour's innovation efforts

Over the years, Carrefour has built up a reputation for being in the forefront of retail technology developments and it has been a frontrunner in introducing technological customer facing retail innovations. Carrefour has piloted and also implemented a wide range of retail technology innovations in the last couple of years. To mention a few:

- Digital walls, and sensors to help customers locate promotions, innovative multiservice terminals, and virtual fitting rooms to enhance and personalize the shopping experience.
- Contactless payment and mobile payment solutions.
- Pikit, the connected device for easy shopping; it enables customers to scan their products so as to add them easily to their online shopping list.
- Home delivery, drive, click & collect, automatic pick-up points, etc.: Carrefour offers customers a complete digitally supported services portfolio for ordering, delivery and collection.
- A connected shopping trolley, with a tablet connected to the trolley push bar, that: shows promotions and discount coupons, digitizes shopping lists, makes products easier to find (thanks to in-store geolocalization), and enables customers to express their preferences and give feedback

Although the above list of retail technologies is already impressive, the most eye-catching retail innovation of recent years certainly has to be the introduction of humanoid robots on the retail shop floor. These friendly human-like machines have up until now mostly acted in a store host role, providing entertainment and information to retail shop customers. The presence of these robots has been successful in the way that they are able to create a unique customer experience touch point; most of the brief encounters result in positive amazement and a smile on the face of the customer.

Robot 'Pepper' - a friendly shop host with a lot of potential

Pepper is produced by SoftBank Robotics and Aldebaran Robotics SAS. Standing 1.20 meters tall, weighing 28 kilograms and making use of four directional microphones, a 10.1-inch touch display, and both a 3D and 2D camera to interact with Carrefour's customers, Pepper is said to be designed to 'make people happy, help them grow, and enhance their lives'. With all the technology on board to support the ability to read the emotions of others, and generate own emotions based on the analysis of expressions and tone of voice, Pepper as a machine is very capable of creating a human-like interaction with people. Additionally, the experiences from a single Pepper are uploaded to a cloud- based Artificial Intelligence system, enabling other units to learn and apply the experiences from a distant unit to their own environment.

The purpose of the humanoid robot Pepper at Carrefour's retail shops

Some examples of the scenarios that can be witnessed in the Carrefour shops are: Pepper...

- ...welcomes customers and provides information via the integrated tablet on its chest about promotions, discounts and the MiCarrefour app.
- ...provides customers with suggested recipes based on a specific ingredient that customers give as input, and subsequently gives directions as where to obtain the ingredients.
- ...initiates interactive play with children through games, dances, selfies and short conversations.
- ...provide customers with the opportunity to give feedback on their shopping experience – by entering a rating on the tablet on its chest.

Carrefour believes that innovation is all about observation and listening to customers. The company further states that there is no better place to find out about customers' expectations, needs and desires, and to test and experiment these, than in the store itself. The introduction of Pepper on the shop floor of the

Carrefour retail stores is completely in line with these beliefs and at the same time it is an excellent example of how two of the cornerstones of Carrefour's retail vision have been brought to life almost literally through the use of technology:

- Combining convenience and enjoyment.
  Making day-to-day life easier by offering choice and quality, and turning shopping into an enjoyable experience: this is what guides our business as a retailer every day.
- Omni-channel and customer experience.
  The customer at the center of the Carrefour ecosystem. Carrefour develops solutions and services to offer the best possible experience to customers in its stores and online.

The effect of Pepper on customer experience metrics

While the introduction of robots in the retail environment at a first glance seems like a step away from the human-centered and personalized approach commonly seen in retail, a closer look reveals quite the opposite. The encounters between Pepper and Carrefour customers can be described as friendly and amusing social interactions, where customers - if they feel the need - can ask questions and request Pepper's assistance. When Pepper suggests recipes based on customer's input and assists customers in finding the required ingredients in the right aisles, it is very clear that the robot triggers a pleasant surprise during the daily groceries routine. An encounter with Pepper is a unique in-store experience that enables Carrefour to make impact during what customers would normally consider a routine activity at best.

The impact of the Carrefour customer-Pepper interactions on brand loyalty and other relational customer experience metrics still need to be measured. However, it is clear that Pepper is able to put a smile on customer's faces, thereby not only boosting the transactional customer satisfaction, but also positively affecting the overall customer relationship.

What your organization can learn from Carrefour:

- The introduction of new technologies in the core processes of your organization should not be standalone decisions, but should be part of an overall strategic innovation and customer experience program.
- Pilot new technologies in the natural environment to get the most reliable and valuable customer response and feedback.
- Dare to try new things. Being at the forefront of customer experience innovation means presenting your customers with truly discerning customer experiences, without having any guarantees on the outcome. At the same time it is a true opportunity to amaze customers, reap their smiles and build your brand as a customer centric organization.
- Ensure your innovations are in line with your organization vision.

ENECO

Agile teams focusing on specific parts of the journey for specific brands

Eneco is one of the largest producers and suppliers of natural gas, electricity and heat in the Netherlands. After the Netherlands, it runs businesses in Great Britain, Germany, France and Belgium. In the highly competitive utility industry, Eneco supplies gas and electricity to the consumer market with four brands:

- Eneco, the biggest mass-market brand.
- Oxxio, the app-only challenger brand.
- WoonEnergie, focusing on tenants through a broad collective of housing corporations.
- Toon, the smart thermostat.

Eneco is continuously focusing on optimizing the customer experience and creating distinctive experiences for each of their brands. Eneco had to switch from simply supplying energy to provide, in their words, 'energy as a service': a broad range of innovative products such as smart energy solutions.

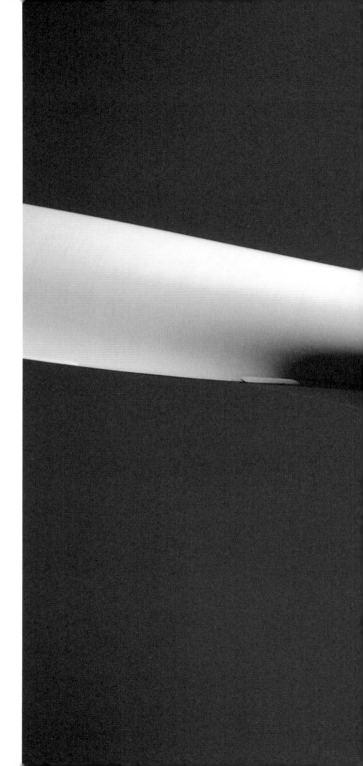

Oxxio: continuously innovating via the app

Oxxio's brand promise is: super smart and super value. With the innovative Oxxio App, customers can gain an insight into their energy consumption and easily arrange all their energy matters themselves with a smartphone or tablet. The app helps consumers to reduce their energy consumption, saving them money. Since the app is central in the customer experience, Oxxio wanted to optimize the customer journey by optimizing the usage of the app.

Inspired by additional mobile touchpoints within other industries such as company apps (mobile banking apps as the clearest example), Oxxio set itself the ambition to create an app-only experience, enabling the customer to have all needed contacts via the app, but moreover, adding further touchpoints throughout the year because of the app.
Oxxio defined five moments within the journey that should make the experience a true Oxxio experience, fitting perfectly with the Oxxio brand. Next to these moments, Oxxio defined additional touchpoints in the journey to create relevant extra contacts. Relevant for the customer, since they should help them to save on their energy consumption, and relevant to Oxxio since they should stimulate usage of the app.

A warm welcome, promoting the app for the customer's benefit

One of these defined Oxxio moments was the start of the relationship: the confirmation of the contract. Oxxio wants their customers to feel welcome from the start. The moment you sign up via Oxxio.nl confetti appears on the website to welcome you. Via the confirmation e-mail all your details are shown as if you are watching them on a tablet and the benefits of using the app are clearly pointed out as well as a text message direct link to the App Store and Google Play to download the app. At the same time, you receive an SMS to welcome you, also mentioning the app to follow the next steps in the process. In case you don't download the app, you'll get a kind reminder some days later mentioning you can easily follow your energy consumption via the app.

In the app, customers can decide how often they want to be remembered to update their energy consumption. This way Oxxio is helping the customers to get a hold on their energy usage, and at the same time Oxxio is building a relationship with the customer by creating additional contacts. Customers rate the app with four stars and customers are more positive on Oxxio after using the app. The usage of the app is growing significantly. Last year the average log-ins per month grew by about 67%! 35% of these contacts don't need to be serviced via the call center anymore. The customers don't need to call, but they can easily find the answer in the app or via the chat function in the app. In one year, Oxxio has decreased costs by over 1 million by dramatically reducing calls and by moving clients from a live call to a social environment. For now the website still exists, but if the current trend continues, Oxxio will probably remove certain web functionalities and only offer them via the app in the future.

Multidisciplinary team to bring new customer-facing initiatives to market rapidly

Oxxio set a clear target audience: the millennials, born between 1980 and 2000, who are price conscious, active online, used to personal approaches and always looking for the best price-quality balance. A dedicated, multidisciplinary team is continuously looking for new ways to serve these millennials even better. This team can quickly anticipate new opportunities that arise in the market.

But Oxxio isn't the only team within Eneco working via the agile principles. Eneco drafted three of these dedicated teams, each with their own business objectives and a clear short-term focus. The goals for each team were to make new customer-facing initiatives live every two weeks which were ideally already tested with customers. This agile way of working was so positive, that within a few months 'illegal' teams copied this methodology, so Eneco decided to bring the whole commercial organization to the next level. The organization designed a truly new, commercial organization with brand teams and customer-oriented missions per team.

These missions are based on the customer journey, to ensure all touchpoints within the journeys are taken care of. Right now, all employees are working according to the same agile method, not only in the commercial department, but also within customer care, back office, credit management and the IT department.

By working in an agile way, the speed of innovation has increased significantly, and customer feedback loops are better embedded than ever, with lower costs and higher customer satisfaction and customer happiness.

What your organization can learn from Eneco:

- Ensure your sub brands all address different target audiences and deliver different experiences.
- Use new technologies especially for those moments that are key to your customers and to your brand.
- Create agile teams with clear non-overlapping focuses to speed up the time to market for innovations.
- Create a positive vibe around a new 'agile' way of working. Others will want to follow.

THE MARRIOTT INTERNATIONAL

Using design thinking to redefine the role of hotels and kickoff internal change

Marriott International Inc. is a leading hospitality multinational with more than 6,000 hotels and lodging facilities in 122 countries and territories and over 1.2 million rooms. This makes the Marriott the largest lodging company based on room count. The American company operates 31 brands differentiating between classic and distinctive brands and ranging from select to luxury brands. Its brands include the Ritz-Carlton, Bulgari Hotels & Resorts, the Sheraton and Westin Hotels. The company was founded by J. Willard and Alice Marriott and guided by family leadership for nearly 90 years. The family helped shape the modern hospitality industry. The Marriott was for instance the first hotel company worldwide to offer guests the option to book reservations online.

Design thinking to reshape and expand Marriott's services

Nowadays Marriott uses design thinking and service design to help redefine the role of a hotel within the total travel experience and the role of hotels in the local community. Design Thinking helps Marriott to think beyond the line of their property and the conventional hotel services. The company designed the Charlotte Marriott City Center as a living lab where the Marriott discovers and tests what customers want and need. As part of the design process the company creates actual characters to experience the new hotel spaces.

The experimental hotel introduced various modern hotel services and areas like a bar and restaurant with an open kitchen to allow for maximum dining experience, a community coffee shop with pop-up or educational events and selling local products and a sophisticated fitness center with on-demand fitness classes and local running routes.

To make check in smooth, informal and personal the front desk has been replaced with check-in tables and employees are able to walk around to greet the guests and to show them around. The various areas, linked to an experimental service, are equipped with feedback buttons to measure what guests like and dislike. Next to these buttons used only at the Charlotte Marriott City Center, the Marriott collects feedback for all its hotels through web analytics, social media, their employees and 20,000 surveys and store reviews per month. Through user feedback, the Marriott for instance learned that guests almost never used their closets, but did prefer a larger television, thus leading to the swap of closet space for a larger TV.

Going digital to support the full guest's journey

Another example of how design thinking helps the Marriott is with the development of their app. The Marriott's app is personalized and reflects the guest's needs at different stages of their stay journey. Based on research on what customers want and their feedback the Marriott builds features and services for different moments.

For instance, if a user has no trips booked the booking bar will be shown on the home screen. However, when a guest opens the app upcoming reservations will be shown and on the day of the trip the app shows content related to the specific hotel. This timed information includes a map and directions, as well as an option to check-in or request services such as extra towels. Guests now utilize the app more for services than merely booking a room, with services making up almost two-thirds of the application usage. To ensure fast development cycles employees from digital and IT are co-located and build features in agile scrum teams.

Experimentation in small teams to generate larger transformations

As a large international organization, developing a strategy for change is challenging. Different divisions across continents need to be on board and existing protocols and processes, which allowed the company to be successful in the first place, need to be overhauled. The Marriott decided to start small, introducing change to fourteen key locations instead of enforcing change top down. They targeted entrepreneurially minded individuals working at their hotels or involved in the local community to come up with innovative ideas. Small teams at each key location were encouraged to experiment with new concepts for food and beverage services that resonated with the local community and the guest. The ideas varied broadly depending on the local preferences and needs.
The London team, for example, opened up a pop-up bar and dinner on the hotel's rooftop, while the Arizona (US) team started a cheese-and-charcuterie restaurant serving artisan cheese and products by local craft beer and wine makers. Through communication of the successes of these small teams the Marriott Management believes greater change can be brought in to the whole company.

What your organization can learn from Marriott International:

- Consider the broader picture, expand the focus beyond the property of the hotel and common hotel services to discover and tap into stated and unstated needs.
- Differentiate between the needs of customers at different stages of the journey and provide relevant information and services to match these needs.
- Collect user feedback to guide decision-making and shape new and current services.
- Start the change with those most willing and open to change, use their success story to incite larger developments.
- Set up experiments to discover what customers like or dislike.

Chapter **5**

BYE-BYE, CUSTOMER EXPERIENCE MANAGER

HOW TO ORGANIZE YOUR CUSTOMER EXPERIENCE MANAGEMENT

Managing the customer experience is not a one-off exercise. You must measure continuously and consistently whether your desired customer experience is actually delivered to your customer and whether your business objectives are met, and act if needed.

Therefore, a customer-centric organization is key. The whole organization should breathe customer experience and align everything in order to deliver the best experience possible. How you should organize your organization to achieve this is what we discuss in this final chapter.

CEX in your organization DNA

How customers perceive your customer experience depends highly on the expectations they have. These expectations are not only set by your organization; on the contrary, they are often set by other companies, even outside your own industry. When other organizations improve their experiences, for example by using new technologies, customers expect the same state-of-the-art experiences from your organization.

And even when other companies would not change anything in their experiences, you still have to optimize yours every now and then. This is because customers get used to the experience you give them. So the first time, you might surprise them and exceed their expectations. The second time, this effect might still be there, but the third and fourth time you won't surprise them anymore and your previously outstanding customer experience has become mediocre.

You should therefore reinvent the customer experience over and over again. How often your journey needs to be refreshed is not a fact. It is highly dependent on your organization's industry, type of product, channels used, and the type of innovations elsewhere. Only by constantly measuring the customer experience can you manage the customer journey and identify when and where action is needed.

The frustrations of the Customer Experience Manager

In order to keep focusing on the customer experiences, most organizations have one or more customer experience managers. Though in title all these roles might seem the same, there are many different customer experience managers. Most often you'll find the customer experience manager somewhere within the commercial department. This is a logical place to find them, since in this area the customer is already at the forefront (or should be, at least). All these managers will agree with us that this works fine for smaller improvements to the customer journey, with no or little involvements from other departments, but that it is harder to get things done when you need to involve IT or operations, for example.

In general, we state that the lower in hierarchy the customer experience manager is placed, the smaller the improvements (and thus the impact) will be, and the more inconsistent the customer journey will be.

In some organizations, the customer experience manager function is, for this reason, part of the organization's board.

These organizations really want to become customer centric and therefore they appoint a person at board level responsible for the total customer experience. This customer experience manager needs to ensure everybody acts with the customer in mind. We applaud this effort. However, if budget allocation takes place, you can imagine it might still be a hard struggle for the customer experience manager to prioritize his or her projects against big cost reduction projects coming from finance, new sales campaigns coming from sales or IT investments coming from IT.

When organizations consider customer experience or customer centricity as something you take care of in projects, we believe this will give the right focus temporarily, but in the long run, the novelty will disappear, and the project will be overshadowed by new projects and thus lose its focus. In our view, an organization can only be truly customer centric and deliver the best customer experience if everybody within the organization feels responsible for the customer experience. To get there, customer experience projects and/or the appointment of customer experience managers might be needed, but we consider them to be temporary. In the end, customer experience is not a role or a function or a project, it should be part of your organization's DNA.

The need for clear customer missions

Fortunately, more and more organizations realize the need for multidisciplinary teams to get things done in the field of customer experience. The agile way of working as described in Chapter 4 is no longer limited to IT projects. Likewise, the commercial part of the organization, we see scrum teams (or other forms of agile teams) made up of people from marketing, communications, online, data, products, operations, IT, etc. Together they are responsible for the customer experience. Will this ensure the best customer experience? Partially, yes. Now there is a multidisciplinary team responsible for the customer experience. They can measure the experience, identify what kind of action is needed and also have the expertise within the team to implement changes and realize the desired experience.

But in most cases this multidisciplinary team is not responsible for the whole customer experience, but for one or a few journeys. For example, one team is responsible for the sales journey and another team for the services. Or one team for the payment journey, another team for movements and a third one for cross-selling. As you can imagine, each individual journey might be perfect, but a consistent customer experience throughout all these individual journeys is harder to realize. In order to create consistency, the design principles as described in Chapter 2 are key. The clearer and more concrete they are, the more consistent the journey will be. Another important driver for consistency are the so-called 'customer missions': the assignments given to the multidisciplinary teams. The level above all these teams, most likely either the commercial management or the board, defines customer missions for each team. The customer missions are mutually exclusive (each team can succeed without interfering with another) and collectively exhaustive (all customer missions together ensure the corporate customer experience strategy is met).

Just as with the design principles, the clearer and more concrete they are, the more consistent the journey will be. For example, the customer mission for the payment team could be 'our customers understand our invoices and are encouraged to pay immediately', and for the movements team 'our customers can easily inform us about their movement and we take care of everything'. Clear and concrete missions, but the first one focuses on transparency and clarity in the journey, whereas the second one is about ease and a hassle-free experience. This could lead to inconsistency for a customer who is moving and then gets a new invoice. Consistency could be secured by changing the customer mission for the movement team into 'our customers understand what they need to do when they are moving'.
Of course, these customer missions should be in line with your brand values. And as stated before, the more distinctive the brand values, the more distinctive the customer experience will be. For example, the brand value 'friendship' may lead to

customer missions like 'our customers are invited to let us know when they have trouble paying our invoice. Together we'll find a solution' and regarding moving: 'our customers let us know when they are moving because they want to. We show our friendship by taking care of everything we can do'.

What about the employee journey?

Clear customer missions help your employees to improve the customer experience in a consistent way. However, what your customers think of your organization is ultimately largely affected by the direct contacts with your employees. Research shows that customers link a good experience to the kindness of the employees, the good service and hospitality. A bad experience is mainly caused by unfriendliness of employees. The role of employees is crucial in the actual customer experience delivered, especially the employees with direct customer contact, since they are the showpiece of your organization. This is particularly true for service providers, where the only physical image a customer gets from your organization may be that of employees. However, employees with no direct contact also indirectly influence the customer experience. When designing the customer journey, it is therefore important to translate this customer journey into the so-called employee journey: a description of the direct and indirect touchpoints the employees have with your customers and what these touchpoints look like. This way, each employee understands their role in the total customer journey and understands what is expected from them.

Of course, the design principles as defined for the customer journey are also an important starting point for the employee journey. However, more important than clear guidelines is the empowerment of employees through the following:

1 The employee breathes the brand and is proud of it.
2 The employee feels responsible for the complete customer experience.
3 The employee has the knowledge and skills to make a difference to the customer.
4 The employee is supported by the organization to act in the best interest of the customer.

 ### The employee breathes the brand and is proud of it

All employees should be true fans of your organization. If you can't manage to make your own employees fan of your brand, how can you ever make your customers fans? Employees should be proud of their job and like it. To attain that, employees should really feel part of your organization. They should understand what your organization does and why. That begins with the primary organization processes, but goes much further. It also involves your policy regarding sustainability or sponsoring, for example.

 ### The employee feels responsible for the total customer experience

The employee should feel responsible for the customer process. Not only for their own role within this, but for the total customer experience. Though the employee journey describes what the organization expects from the employee, there should be enough degrees of freedom for the employee to define what is truly needed at that moment to best help the customer. By giving the employee enough autonomy to make their own judgments, they can help the customer better. Moreover, this makes the job of the employee far more motivating and stimulating.

 ### The employee has the knowledge and skills to make a difference to the customer

Of course, the employee should have the right knowledge to help the customer, such as knowledge about the product and processes. The right skills are, however, just as important: listening, being helpful, feeling empathetic, understanding and being responsive are important for employees with direct customer contact. These skills are not always easy to train, since they are part of of a person's character. Attracting and recruiting the right employees for direct customer contacts is very important, but often not enough attention is paid to this.

4 *The employee is supported by the organization to act in the best interest of the customer*

Lastly, the organization should create the right circumstances for the employee to do their job in the best way. By this, we mean that the right processes and systems should be in place, but also the right management and key performance indicators (KPIs). For example, it is really hard for employees with direct customer contact to deliver the best customer experience when they are encouraged to spend as little time on the phone as possible. Or to push as many products to the customer as possible. Fortunately, within the customer contact department we see a shift towards KPIs like NPS instead of average handling time or sales.

The four prerequisites for employees as described here might make you think we believe organizations should not outsource their customer contacts. But that is not true. We strongly believe the same excellent customer experience can be delivered both with your own employees or outsourcing partners. As long as you make sure the above four preconditions are taken into account.

Align with your total ecosystem

We already touched upon the subject of outsourcing. Whether you outsource or not, there will always be 'partners' that are part of your customer journey. Together they all form your customer experience ecosystem and should support the customer experiences you want to deliver. Think about the mailman delivering your product to the customer. They are not part of your organization, but if the package is delivered damaged, the customer will probably call you and not the mail company. Another good example is the customer journey of a car insurance claim. From the insurer's point of view, this customer journey roughly consists of making the claim, sharing the details and receiving the money. However, from the customer's point of view, the journey is far more complicated and consists also of touchpoints such as finding a garage, making an appointment and getting a replacement vehicle. When the customer is not satisfied with the garage, they will be disappointed in the total claim journey, which will also affect the insurer.

To map your total customer experience ecosystem, always make sure you map the customer journey from the customer's point of view and find out which parties are involved in that journey.

The effect of outsourcing on the customer experience

Sometimes, these partners will work under your organization's name and the customer won't know they are not actually part of your organization. But sometimes the customer will notice the different organizations. What is the effect of having partners on the customer experience? Which partners to choose? Together with the Center for Marketing Leadership of Vrije Universiteit, Amsterdam, we are investigating the effect of outsourcing to another brand on the customer experience. The first preliminary outcomes of our research show that when companies outsource their negative contact moments, for example, contacts around lost luggage for an airline company, the customer experience with that company is evaluated more positively than if they had taken care of these negative contact moments themselves. Outsourcing negative contact moments is beneficial for your customer experience, as long as these contacts are not related to the core business of your organization.

But to whom is it best to outsource to? Should it be a strong or a weak brand? It turns out that if the outsourced moment leads to a negative experience (for example the delivery of a damaged package) it is better if the subcontractor is a weak brand.

The customer will link the negative experience in that case to the weak brand of the organization outsourced to and not to yours. Since the customer will already have had no or low expectations from the weak brand, the experience is completely in line with this. If the company outsourced to had been a strong brand, the negative experience would not be in line with what the customer was expecting and the negative experience is in that case linked to the outsourcing company. If the outsourced moment leads to a positive experience, it doesn't matter whether the subcontractor is a strong or a weak brand.

Figure 5.1 Preconditions for a successful partnership

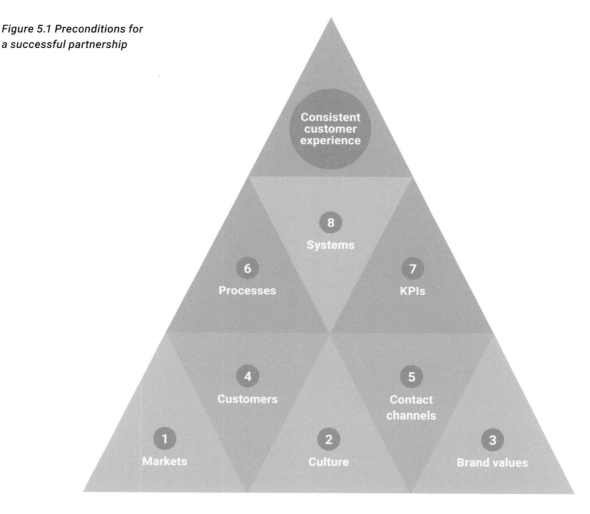

Although our research on the effects of outsourcing is still ongoing, the first results show outsourcing negative contact moments to a weak brand is from a customer experience point of view the best option. Moreover, this will probably be the cheaper option too.

Nonetheless, companies should be very careful to select a weak brand to handle the contact moments. When trust is an important element in the customer journey, a strong brand might be a better option. Take 'payments' as an example. This is in general a negative moment for the customer. Yet it is crucial in the sales journey, since without a good payment, the customer might not even become your customer. In that case a strong brand that can guarantee a flawless payment process would be preferable.

Next to deciding on a strong or a weak brand, we believe all partners in the customer experience ecosystem should ideally be more or less identical. The more the partners look alike, the more consistent the customer experience will be. We differentiate eight preconditions for a successful partnership:

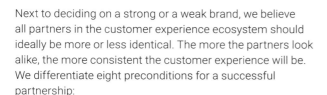

1 Does the partner focus on the same markets?

2 Does the partner have an identical internal culture?

3 Does the partner have the same brand values?

4 Does the partner target identical customers?

5 Does the partner use the same contact channels?

6 Does the partner use matching processes?

7 Does the partner measure the same key performance indicators (KPIs)?

8 Does the partner use identical systems?

The more of these answers can be answered with 'yes', the closer a partner is to your organization and the more consistent the customer experience will be.

These nine prerequisites for a consistent customer experience make a pyramid. The higher you get in the pyramid, the tougher it gets to answer the questions with 'yes'.

Key take-aways:

- In order to be truly customer centric, customer experience should not be a role, function or project, but embedded in your organization DNA.
- Clear customer missions ensure teams within your organization will all work towards a consistent customer experience.
- Special attention should be paid to the employees with direct customer contact, to enable them to deliver the right customer experience directly.
- When outsourcing contacts, make a well-informed decision as to whether to outsource to a strong or a weak brand.
- Look for partners that are like your own organization to create a successful customer experience ecosystem.

FIETSKOERIERS.NL

A new way of delivering packages

Fietskoeriers.nl is an ambitious Dutch startup company, delivering packages by bike (fietskoerier means bike courier in Dutch). It started delivering in May 2016 and delivered around 50,000 packages in 2016. This year Fietskoeriers.nl is estimating a total number of deliveries of 1 million. If they succeed, Fietskoeriers.nl will have grown 2000% in just 1.5 years. Right now Fietskoeriers.nl has 550 employees delivering for 18 different companies in 29 cities but that is not their only goal. Fietskoeriers.nl wants to be the only delivery company delivering in cities. They want to move all cars out of the city in order to improve the environment and protect people from exhaust fumes. Cars would only be allowed to drive outside cities from warehouses to the hubs outside the city. Bikes would then finish the job and take the package into the city.

Most ecofriendly delivering company is a clear competitive advantage

Fietskoeriers.nl is a platform for companies that deliver purchases by bike from online web shops in the Netherlands. Delivering only by bike they are the most environmentally friendly delivery company in the Netherlands. Any webshop can join Fietskoeriers.nl for delivering packages. If a customer buys a product at an online shop which is a client of Fietskoeriers. nl, the package is either picked up by a delivery person by bike, if the delivery is in the same town, or picked up by a car if the delivery is in another city. The car drives to a 'hub' at the edge of the city where another bike courier will take the package and deliver it.

In this way every package is delivered by bike in the end. Why use bikes? Bikes are cheaper and more sustainable but also faster. A deliverer is much faster in cities due to the agility and mobility of a bike. The fact that every last mile of the delivery is done by bike saves a lot of traffic and a lot of exhaust fumes in cities. Bikes can also park in front of every door so the delivery schedule leaves more room to make the customer happy.

98% of the packages are successfully delivered because of more flexibility than competitors

Delivery by bike the way Fietskoeriers.nl does it is ideal for the customer. Fietskoeriers.nl gives a track and trace code to every customer informing him or her of the estimated delivery time. The customer then knows when the package will arrive so they can make sure they're home. If they know he can't make it in time for the delivery there is an option to contact the delivery guy. The delivery guy can just change his route and stop by the park for instance if the customer is there. This way the customer also feels like he himself is helping the environment and his neighbors by letting his package arrive by bike and not by car.

The second reason for success is that Fietskoeriers.nl does deliveries in the evening past 6 pm. This increases the chance of a successful delivery because most people are already home

from their jobs. This way 98% of the packages are successfully delivered the first time. Every customer wants his package as soon as possible so this is great for the customers.

The use of bikes enables Fietskoeriers.nl to use smarter routes that make it possible to deliver more packages in the same time as that of a bus or a car. The motorized vehicles need to tank fuel, stay on roads that are built for cars, deal with traffic and have a higher percent chance of an accident that keeps the driver from continuing his delivery.

All employees are really motivated creating an excellent experience

Last but not least, Fietskoeriers.nl will do anything to make the delivery special. Though everyone in the Netherlands knows how to ride a bike, the people delivering for Fietskoeriers. nl are highly educated people with a strong will to make the customer happy. The job is a well-paid job with great chances of making a career in the entire company. For example: over 50% percent of the people working at the office of Cycloon (owner of Fietskoeriers.nl) used to be a deliverer for Fietskoeriers.nl. Because of these advantages Fietskoeriers.nl receives a lot of applications but only 10 percent gets a job. This is because Fietskoeriers.nl only takes those applicants that are really motivated to make the customer happy. This is tested in the two days of test-delivering. If the applicant does not manage to cycle the entire day or evening and stay customer focused, he does not get the job. This way Fietskoeriers.nl secures its position as a customer focused company.

What your organization can learn from Fietskoeriers.nl:

- Find the deeper customer insights and build your proposition around them.
- Define what you expect from your employees and be selective in the recruitment process. Only people who are intrinsically motivated can help you build up your organization.
- Be creative in internal processes and allow employees to overrule if this benefits the customer.
- Customer experience at Fietskoeriers.nl is no role, function or project but embedded in the organization DNA.

USAA

Knows what it means to serve

USAA (United Services Automobile Association) was established in 1922 by a group of US army officers, who discovered that it was difficult for them to secure car insurance owing to the perception that being US officers, they belonged to a 'high-risk' group. These officers agreed to take a different approach and self-insure each other: the United Services Automobile Association was born. Today USAA offers banking, investing and insurance to people and families who serve, or served, in the US army. USAA is still member-owned and refers to its customers as members.

Employees are a success factor for great experiences

The USAA members are the starting point of every decision made within the company. The slogan 'We know what it means to serve' clearly reflects the audience they target, but also their never-ending focus on customer experiences. Though USAA does not have any physical branches, they make it easy for members to contact them. USAA uses all remote channels available, such as mail, telephone, ATM machines and internet. One of the success factors of great experiences via all these channels is the employees. The training USAA gives to its employees is close to a military experience; they even receive army food rations, for instance, helping them get into the members' mindset so they can best 'serve' them.

The introduction of new channels such as the mobile devices made USAA realize that if they wanted to continue to remotely serve their members in the best way, they also had to respond quickly to new innovations.

Organizational structure designed for innovation and superior customer service

Not only did they have to add new channels, they also found out that their growing number of products and services offered via those channels led to increasing complexity. Different business lines all managed their own touchpoints and for the customer this silo approach often led to situations where customers had to contact different departments to get things done.

In order to make it much easier for its members, USAA redesigned its organizational structure around them. Instead of taking the products as the starting point, they defined life events with significant financial impact for the members, such as buying a house, becoming a parent or retiring from the army. Each of these life events causes new financial needs that typically involve products and services across the different business lines.

A new business unit was created to deliver this integrated experience across products, services and channels: the Member Experience (MX) unit. Within this unit all service agents, channel managers, marketing and sales reps now work together on the best member experiences for each life event. An executive vice president, directly reporting to the CEO, leads the unit. Now all member-facing employees are brought together within MX, providing the members with one contact point for when needed. Training the employees across products was key in order to deliver the integrated experience to the customer. Bundling all customer contacts in one new unit also made the path free for the different product lines to focus on product innovation. And since they can never market these products without contacting the members, they always have to collaborate with MX. Multidisciplinary cooperation and integrated solutions are the result.

However, this new structure also made it clear that there were a lot of interdependencies between the different departments. In order to speed up the decision-making process between these departments, special decision making forums were introduced. And even though USAA started implementing the new structure as of 2010, they are still learning and improving to keep up with the pace of the market.

Technology designed to make customers feel better protected

Today USAA is well known for its technological innovations, continuously matching the technical possibilities with the customer's true needs. As an example, USAA understands that it can be hard for US officers serving abroad to keep an eye on their finances. To address this need, USAA has developed a mobile service that enables individuals to simply text USAA and their account number to USAA and then receive a reply message that informs them of their current balance. Next to this they offer a cloud-based mobile application, using social media technology to help the members stay in touch with their families back home.

New financial technologies, such as biometric authentication, enables smartphone users to get access to their accounts by voice recognition or even eye-scanning technologies, extra security to make the members feel better protected and truly looked after.
USAA scores high on various customer experience rankings and their NPS scores are comparable with, and often even higher than, Apple and Amazon.

What your organization can learn from USAA:

- Use your organization's mission as a starting point in everything you do. "We know what it means to serve", declares USAA.
- Put the customer at the forefront for every decision you make.
- Organize the business around the customer and their journeys; traditional functions will become less relevant.
- Dare to start restructuring your business and make changes later to continuously optimize it.
- Train and inspire your employees with your organization's mission.
- Always keep on innovating to meet and exceed your customer's expectations.

MORNING STAR

Self-management beyond empowerment

Morning Star is the largest tomato processor company in the United States. Based in California, the company supplies approximately 40% of the U.S. industrial tomato paste and diced tomato markets. Morning Star has over $700 million in annual revenues and numbers close to 400 employees. However, it does not speak about employees: instead, it refers to them as 'colleagues' since the organization strongly believes in the principles of self-management.

Employees work independently and make job decisions themselves

Morning Star was built on the foundations of self-management: everyone is responsible for coordinating themselves with fellow colleagues, customers and partners in their ecosystem, with no orders from others. The whole enterprise is organized around the idea that there are no human bosses in the organization. Instead, the company mission statement is the boss. Colleagues are encouraged to work independently and to make job decisions themselves, naturally in consultation with experts. Morning Star firmly believes its colleagues find joy and excitement when they use their unique talents and are able to weave those talents into activities which complement and strengthen the activities of their colleagues. All colleagues are personally responsible and hold themselves accountable for the success of this self-management.

Self-management and transparency is key

However, self-management does not mean there are no guidelines. Values, accountability and systems are embedded in the Morning Star culture to ensure self-management works. So how does this work in practice?
Since Morning Star moved from a hierarchical to a networked management structure, networks are not built on orders from top management, but on peer-to-peer agreements.
Each Morning Star colleague and business unit develops individual mission statements. These statements are a concretization of the company mission statement and create the framework for their job. Then, every year, each colleague and business unit together develops 'Colleague Letters of Understanding (CLOUs)' that describe how they will work with others: personal missions, roles and responsibilities, process management etc. Furthermore, it describes how to measure the outcome by defining the relevant key performance indicators (KPIs, what they call 'Stepping stones').

The Colleague Letters of Understanding are formal, explicit commitments. Just like a contract, these CLOUs are signed. Originally the CLOU was on paper, but nowadays it is online.

All CLOUs are available to the whole company, since in order to hold each other accountable, transparency is key.
Data, both on individual performances and on company level, is shared frequently. This data not only gives an opportunity to reflect on previous decisions made, but more importantly it enables all colleagues to make the best decisions for the future. Next, qualitative feedback from peer reviews is shared to improve accountability.

No bosses, but colleagues are involved in decisions

All commitments are peer-to-peer, not top-down. Anyone in Morning Star has the authority to spend money and hire new colleagues, as long as they can justify those actions to their peers. The bigger the decision, the more colleagues need to be involved in this decision to ensure commitment.
Next to empowerment, there are also restrictions to self-management. Since there are no bosses, people cannot be fired. No colleague can simply dismiss a fellow colleague by himself. At the same time, nobody can tell another colleague what to do.

Within Morning Star leadership is earned

Though Morning Star might not have a formal hierarchy, there are many informal ones. And these hierarchies are dynamic, based on relative influence. Within Morning Star leadership is earned, not conveyed by position or title. Because of expertise and willingness to help fellow colleagues, one colleague may have a bigger say than others. So authority comes from helping peers, demonstrating expertise and thus adding value. CLOUs evolve from year to year to reflect changing expertise and shifting interests. More experienced colleagues take on more complex tasks and thrust more basic tasks to new colleagues. As a result, Morning Star colleagues who are within the company for a longer time have a broader expertise than they would have gotten elsewhere.

As you can imagine, this system does not work for all people. People who like to be dominant and to give orders to others, cannot survive at Morning Star. At the same time, people who lack initiative can't be successful either. Especially for new hires with previous work experience in more traditional companies, adapting to the Morning Star system is quite a change. Morning Stars focuses heavily on attracting colleagues who embrace the values of self-management. All colleagues receive training on self-management every two years.

Everyone takes responsibility for innovation

Since everyone has the right to suggest improvements anywhere, Morning Star colleagues often drive change outside their own department. Everyone feels responsible to take the lead in innovations in any area where their skills might add value. Morning Star launches hundreds of change initiatives every year in order to make the lives of their customers better through cost effectiveness, excellent service and the best customer support. And successfully, too: over the past 20 years volumes, revenues and profits of the company have all shown double-digit growth, though the average growth within the industry was 1% per year.

What your organization can learn from Morning Star:

- Maximize collaboration with all partners within your eco-system by empowering employees to do what they believe is best.
- Set clear frameworks for the self-managed teams to guide how people work together.
- Ensure everyone feels responsible for the customer experience and provide employees with a culture that empowers them to always act in the best interest of the customer.

VOLVO

Customer experience innovation driven by shifts in the customer profile

The Volvo Car Group is a Swedish car manufacturer owned by the Chinese Geely Group. Volvo Cars, with headquarters in Gothenburg, employs about 30,000 people, has production facilities in Sweden, Belgium and China with the US soon to follow. Volvo Cars sells its products in more than 100 markets. In 2016, the Volvo Car Group's net sales amounted to close to €19 billion, with a volume of 534,000 cars.

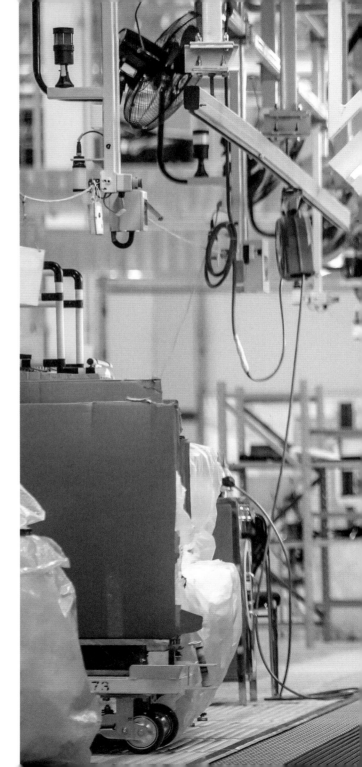

Digital revolution transformed Volvo from B2B to B2C

The automotive industry is quite traditional. The ecosystem consists of many logistical parties: from factory to wholesaler to dealership. Often, a leasing company is also one of the links in the total chain. Until recently, Volvo was B2B-oriented, in line with the existing ecosystem and value chain.

With the rapid rise of the internet, consumers were able to get closer to Volvo in the digital world. By searching for car specifics, using configurators and comparison sites, consumers are starting their customer journey online. The orientation phase of the customer journey is no longer restricted to dealerships since there is a mass of information (reviews, specs, videos) available online. Volvo realized that they were starting a genuine, continuous dialog with consumers. They were becoming B2C instead of B2B.

From silo approach to central customer experience focus

The shift from B2B to B2C requested a different organizational approach. Like many large organizations, Volvo had several siloes which all had some sort of customer interaction, but they all focused on different targets. This resulted in a suboptimal customer experience. Global Marketing focused on generating leads and creating buzz, sales focused on closing deals and Operations was mainly concerned with optimizing operation costs. One can imagine how these different KPIs do not result in the best customer experience.

Volvo created a new unit, the 'Global Customer Experience' group, in which a great customer experience was the most important KPI. The team is run by a senior vice president who reports directly to the global CEO.

This team identifies customer journeys with all touchpoints, both online and offline, and searches for pains and gaps and tries to resolve these in cooperation with other departments. The strategy and vision created by the Global Customer Experience team is executed by the other departments. The biggest gap is found between the online and offline orientation

in the customer journey. A consumer searches online for a car and compares all types of brands and features. When the consumer finally decides to go to a dealership selling their preferred brand, he or she is already far ahead in the customer journey. But the sales rep in the dealership treats the consumer as 'just started his or her customer journey' by asking the very broad question "what can I help you with", thus resulting in the consumer having to explain all of their research. Ideally, the sales rep would know the search history and important criteria and would elaborate on this. Volvo cars is currently running the first pilots on this.

The Global Customer Experience team motivates all other departments to look 'outside in' instead of their traditional 'inside out' approach. Despite the central organization of this team, Volvo clearly proclaims that CEX is not to be centralized. It is not the responsibility of just one department, just as quality is not a centralized responsibility.

CIO becomes Customer Experience Officer

With the explosive use of their online channels, Volvo realized that IT and marketing had become very close. That is why Volvo is consolidating the consumer interface (run by IT) and the business into one department. IT used to be seen as a support function, but is now seen as part of the commercial process. The boundaries between IT and the business are broken down. The CIO might one day become the Customer Experience Officer, since Volvo thinks that IT is taking a frontrunner-role in customer experience in the digital world.

CEO wants his customers to have the same experience as himself

In one of the board meetings, the CEO of Volvo had an epiphany. He stated, "I want my customers to have the same experience as I have. My car is always clean, and I can get a car whenever and wherever I want to. I never feel limited by my car". With this vision in mind, Volvo created the Volvo Concierge Services and launched a pilot in San Francisco. By using so-called digital keys, the app Volvo has developed which enables car owners to 'share' their car usage with other parties, cars can get cleaned and filled up, so their owners don't have to worry about these time-consuming tasks. Volvo wants to free up time for their customers to do what they want to do!

Volvo realizes that the automotive branch is not the frontrunner in customer experience. That is why they seek inspiration across branches. The travel industry has provided them with new ideas; the seamlessness of finding travel ideas, booking a trip across many different organizations (flight agencies, car rentals, hotels) inspires Volvo to reduce pain points in their customer journey and to partner up with parties in their ecosystem. They want their consumers to get the same seamless experience. In an ideal world, Volvo would like their customers and potential customers to be able to configure their car online and book a test-drive at a time that suits them (most likely in the evenings). The car of their choice should be delivered to their house or office, so the consumer can test-drive it without the hassle of going to a dealership.

What your organization can learn from Volvo:

- Customer experience should not be the responsibility of just one person or department. Make it a shared responsibility, just as quality is.
- Identify all pain points looking at the total customer journey across channels, both on- and offline, and throughout the ecosystem. Think of wholesalers, retailers, presence on partner-websites etc.
- Bridge the gap between IT and Marketing by defining shared responsibilities regarding the customer experience.
- Get inspiration from organizations outside your own industry.

ZHONG AN

China's first internet-based insurance company

Zhong An was founded in 2013 when three big Chinese companies from different industries decided to join forces and cooperate on developing digital insurance services and products. Ping An, a big insurance incumbent from China, is one of its founders. Tencent, a Chinese tech firm mostly known for its famous instant messaging platform WeChat, is another founder. E-commerce superpower Alibaba is the third party involved. The digital insurer they've created together aims to disrupt the insurance sector by applying digital strategies to insurance and fully digitizing the insurance products themselves and the distribution and claims handling processes involved.

Combining industry expertise and customer bases to disruption the insurance industry

By combining the expertise from their three distinctive industries and their massive customer bases, Zhong An has been able to rapidly create new and unique digital insurance services and products.

Within four years, the company has built a portfolio of 300+ digital insurance products and services covering product quality, seller credibility, after-sales services, transaction safety, consumer finance, and health among others. Examples are its Return Insurance covering the costs of shipping returned online goods, Cargo Insurance covering damage of shipped online goods and its Flight Delay Insurance, offering delayed travelers discount coupons when delayed at the airport.

Being present in micro-moments of the customer journey

An important pillar of Zhong An's strategy is its customer-centric approach to delivering digital insurance services. The insurer aims to offer the right insurance solution during a small, but obvious pain point in the customer's buying journey. Take for example a customer ordering a pair of shiny shoes for his girlfriend's birthday through Tmall.com, doubting if she will really like the color he chooses.

His doubt about the color he picks is a tiny detail in his buying process, although this micro-moment is a real moment of truth in deciding whether to buy his present online or look out for alternatives. A big deal in the Chinese e-commerce market, where clothing makes up the largest share of online goods sold and returned.

By offering a Return Insurance as an integral part of the customer's buying journey, customer doubts can be easily overcome since shipping costs for potential return (and exchange) are covered by Zhong An's insurance. The result is a win-win-win situation:

First of all, customers get a seamless and integral shopping experience and can effortlessly insure potential online purchase risks, at negligible cost.

Second, as a result of its 'plug-in' distribution model, e-commerce players can easily integrate these micro-services in their platforms to improve customer service and experience and create new sources of revenue through commissions on sold insurance policies.

Third, by integrating itself in the customer buying journey and the eco-system of e-commerce players (instead of creating an online distribution channel itself), Zhong An enables itself to scale its distribution exponentially at marginal costs.

Moving towards the customer and pulling customers in through the eco-system

The company's most outstanding and skyrocketing result to date, underlining the success of its strategy, is its sales record during China's Singles' Day (one of the biggest shopping days in the world, with 17.6 billion US dollars worth of goods being sold online). Through integration of its Return Insurance in China's major e-commerce platforms like Tmall.com, Zhong An sold 210 million policies of its Return Insurance offering its customers costless shipment of returns, resulting in almost 2 billion dollars of revenue in a single day.

This is where the real business opportunity comes from for digital micro-service providers like Zhong An: by integrating itself in the customer's buying journey and in the eco-system of e-commerce platforms, Zhong An moves towards its customers instead of pulling customers in through its own distribution channels. The network-effect created results in exponential scaling of its distribution power and volumes sold, resulting in significant growth in customer numbers. Initially, these customers only buy a single micro-insurance, but as a result of huge volumes in the network and potential future cross- and upsell opportunities on acquired customers, Zhong An reaps great benefits from their customer-centric, networked strategy.

What your organization can learn from Zhong An:

- Insurance is a means to an end for customers. Therefore insurers must start looking for the real pain points generating customer demand and start integrating their products at natural, relevant moments in the customer's journey.
- By offering its products as 'plug-ins' instead of standalone products, Zhong An enables its network of partners to easily integrate Zhong An's services and leverages the eco-system to boost its distribution.
- Micro-insurance like Zhong An's Return Insurance are low-margin products. By combining these low-margin, micro-services with the exponential distribution power of partner networks, companies can create huge sales volumes resulting in significant revenue potential.
- Taking a headstart in the digital insurance marketplace offered Zhong An significant mover advantage, which makes it difficult for incumbent competitors and new entrants to compete with Zhong An and take away market share.

SCOTCH & SODA

Consistent experiences worldwide via an online academy

Scotch & Soda is a Dutch fashion company founded in the 1980s, but largely rebranded and relaunched in 2001. Scotch and Soda manufactures premium and upmarket men's clothing as well as women's clothing under the brand Maison Scotch, boys' clothing under Scotch Shrunk, girls' clothing under Scotch R'Belle, denim and urban products under Amsterdams Blauw and a line of fragrances named Barfly. It has over 150 stores, and can be found in over 8,000 other locations including the best global department-stores and independents, as well as on several online fashion platforms.

A unique set of core values
The fashion brand started as very 'rough', exploring an 'outlaw' type of brand, focusing on independence and breaking the rules. Designers are encouraged to travel the world and come back with ideas. Each garment has its own story and external influence, which might be visible in the washing, the fit or the pattern.

As the brand grew, it became a bit more accessible. In their own words: "Creativity. Combinations. Influences from around the world. Young. Headstrong. Informal. Pleasure and Expertise. By and for the people". This is summarized in three brand values:
- Eclectic
- Playful
- Rebellious

The brand values are represented in the organizational culture as well. Employees are sincerely interested in each other and new ideas are openly welcomed. They are supported to try out new things quickly and it is okay to fail, and try again. And of course, these brand values are also transferred to the customer experience.

Employees as mannequins
The in-store employees play a crucial part in the customer journey. Each employee has multiple 'functions': this ranges from inspiring customers with the clothes they wear (there are no mannequins in-store), to keeping the store in order, to advising customers and giving them the feeling that they are buying more than just a garment. Everyday before the store opens, employees discuss a certain topic, such as the new collection, low sellers etc.
For the styling part, there are three important guidelines:
- Dare to express.
- Have necessary knowledge.
- Offer golden advice in outfits and combinations.

Employees are supported to welcome each customer and have some small talk, unrelated to fashion. All of these tips and tricks are taught in the Scotch Academy.

The Scotch Academy is an online platform, which functions both as a training platform and an intranet. Via the platform, the head offices communicate with the employees worldwide and information about the brand, new ideas and general marketing is provided on it. Besides this, ideas for morning sessions and quizzes to test your Scotch and Soda knowledge are provided. The goal is to keep the in-store employees up-to-date, make them feel part of the family and create a distinctive and recognizable customer experience wherever the customer is shopping. Working at Scotch & Soda is not just a side job: it is much more. Employees can achieve different (stylist) levels and develop themselves.

Decentralizing as part of the central strategy
Since every town and location is different, consumers never have the exact same experience. Scotch & Soda uses this characteristic and expands it into a true experience. Store employees are encouraged to know a lot about the city their shop is located in, and provide their customers with tips and tricks for a nice experience outside of the store.

In Amsterdam, they took this one step further by creating a city guide (printed, as well as in app-form) called "The Misguiding Guide of Amsterdam". In this book, several typical Amsterdam characters (including several Dutch celebrities) were interviewed about how they like to get lost in the city. This results in many funny and interesting tips which you will not find in any other city guide.

What your organization can learn from Scotch & Soda:

- Freedom for your employees results in greater creativity and more value. Let your employees find inspiration on tours and travel.
- Use internal employee training to develop your employees, and also to keep knowledge and DNA equal among all employees.
- Physical 'offline' stores tend to receive less attention due to the online retail battle. However, people still live in an offline world, so paying attention to a great offline experience can pay off, even when the rest of your branch is focusing mainly on online.

ACKNOWLEDGEMENTS

CEX Sells is based on our vast experiences within the field of customer experience. In our consultancy work at VODW we have supported over 100 organizations worldwide in optimizing their customer experience. All these optimized customer journeys are a treasured source of inspiration.
All content is based on public sources. Where possible, we checked and enriched the content with the organizations mentioned in the book.

CEX Sells could not have been written without the help of many of our colleagues.
In particular, we would like to thank:
Roelie Bottema, Marcel van Brenk, Stephen Fiedeldeij, Astrid Geerlings, Marvin Gommans, Nienke Gruppelaar, Robin Hagen, Mark Hoskam, Richard Kamst, Ronald de Kimpe, Michael Klazema, Anne Kranzbuhler, Dries Laurs, Suzanne Legtenberg, Marjon van der Maat, Rogier Moens, Carli Mollema- Witteveen, Lotte Noordermeer, Paul Peters, Roger Peverelli, Patrick Ruijs, Maton Sonnemans, Brenda Steens, Stijn Toonen, Michel van der Wal, Kim Westerweel, Eduard de Wilde and Jurre Witte.
Many thanks to you all!

We would also like to thank Bionda Dias and Sara van de Ven from BIS Publishers for their support and patience,
Boris Rijksen for his great design work and Phoebe Blackburn for the thorough final edit.
And last but not least, we would like to thank our family and friends for their never-ending support!